Robin,
Let curosity be your
North Star and celebrate
life in all its forms. ~~Pat~~

BLOWING THE INCENSE
FROM YOUR EYES

Awakening the Courage to Implement Personal
and Institutional Reform in the Catholic Church

Patrick Westerhouse

ISBN-10: 147015949X
ISBN-13: 9781470159498
Library Of Congress Control Number: 2012903895
CreateSpace, North Charleston, South Carolina

Cover design by Jeanine Earnhart

DEDICATION

To Patti
You have brought love and wisdom to my life,
and enlightened the journey we have walked together.

To injured Catholics everywhere:
may these words bring healing.

To my creative Muse within: remind me
to love unconditionally.

CONTENTS

ACKNOWLEDGMENTS

The words on these pages are the result of the gifts of many contributors whose wisdom, patience and loving support brought this book to life.

To Mal Costa, a friend of forty years, whose editing of content and writing style, along with his enthusiastic support, kept me at the keyboard to finish the manuscript when I no longer saw its value. Both Mal and my client and friend Will Sousae blessed the final content and encouraged me to take on the largest international organization in the world. Thank you—I think.

To Mike Holden who encouraged and fed me critical feedback over many a breakfast of eggs and sausage. And to his wife, Linda, whose support and contacts saved a ton of time in getting the book published, and opened doors so the work could find its way to the marketplace.

To Jeanine Earnhart, artist, writer, and new friend, who shared stories of early Catholic insanity with humor and grace. Your contact and experience with the world of self-publishing was very helpful, and your artistry on creating the cover catches the eye and communicates the focus of this work.

To Dick and Ann Walenta, whose feedback and insights on Christianity, Buddhism, and wisdom literature enlighten all who cross their paths. Aloha!

To Mary Ann Tyson and Mike Westerhouse, who "think outside the box" and have brought connections and ideas to the book that I was unable to see.

To Jane Halloran for her feedback, love, and support. She has walked the path from Catholic to Christian with grace and humor, and the Church is better for it.

To Gail Petersen, whose wisdom about teams and her courage to engage life as she finds it have been a beacon for working through the challenges of completing the work.

To Jack and Barbara Tooley, who asked critical questions at the beginning of the writing that focused the work. Their encouraging feedback after reading the first, clumsy draft left me with the energy and desire to go forward.

To my wife, Patti, whose love, patience, and forbearance have been incredibly important in bringing this book to fruition as I retreated to the cave of my thoughts and feelings over the past year. Your skill with the computer and your ability to work with the publishing demands made it all possible and worthwhile.

Finally, to all those clergy, religious, and laypeople working in the institutional vineyard who have remained faithful to the Gospel message in serving the People of God. Your example in words and deeds is what keeps the message alive in the communities you serve.

INTRODUCTION

FROM CATHOLIC TO CHRISTIAN: MY NECESSARY JOURNEY

*My very top priority is for people to understand that they have
the power to change things themselves.*
— Aung San Suu Kyi; Burma Activist
and Nobel Peace Prize winner

It was September 1968, and I was returning to Catholic
University in Washington, D.C., where I was to complete
my final year of studies before ordination to the Catholic
priesthood. Since I had been ordained a Deacon in April,
I was wearing the traditional Roman collar associated with
priests. I boarded the plane and took my seat next to a man
who, I would discover later, was a Muslim from the Middle
East.

After exchanging the usual pleasantries regarding desti-
nation and reason for travel, he motioned to the collar and
asked, "Are you a Christian?"

Without hesitation I responded, "No, I'm Catholic."

His immediate follow-up question was, "What's the difference?"

I was stunned into silence. Not because I couldn't explain the distinctions between religious tradition and Christian faith, but that I identified myself as Catholic when he clearly asked if I was Christian. Why wasn't my response, "Yes, I'm a Christian, and my tradition is Catholic within the Christian community of believers"?

I realized that throughout my early life up through ordination in 1969, I was schooled to be Catholic. In my family, school, and church affiliations, the emphasis was Catholic first, with all the rites and rituals, rules and regulations controlled by men who exercised unquestioned power and authority over the spiritual lives of their Catholic parishioners, as well as over their status in the Church community. I had been indoctrinated and subsequently ordained to serve an institution that expected that canon law and conservative positions on difficult life issues would supersede the gospel message of non-judgment, love, and forgiveness. This gospel proclaims, encourages, and holds the individual to be the responsible agent in exploring what it means to grow as a loving human being.

That brief airplane interaction began a challenging reflection that, along with significant conflict with my bishop and pastor concerning issues of pastoral importance—for example, the exclusion of people from sacramental life because of marital status or family planning options—led to my realization that the Church was first organizationally Catholic and secondarily Christian.

In the confessional, in the counseling office, and at the bedsides of dying patients, I listened to people express their challenges and struggles with the expectation that I, as a representative of the Church, would provide answers for the most serious of life's mysteries. The options for consolation were paltry, ranging from the rules and regulations of canon law, to the need for more faith, to the one that implied: God wouldn't give you a burden you couldn't handle—which implies that, if you weren't handling it, there's something lacking in you. As you will see later, the inadequacy was mine, and one that I would struggle with during my priesthood because I was trying to solve a problem that didn't belong to me.

What do I mean by "the Church is first Catholic and then Christian"? Throughout its history, the organizational Church and its bishops and priests have been protected at the expense of the people they serve. The history of the Inquisition, the current history of the abuse scandals, and numerous examples in between validate this assertion. That mandate for survival has allowed for physical abuse and quelled dissent. It has also alienated those willing to serve as priests, especially women, and isolated from Catholic communities those not adhering to the rules and regulations.

As a result, when threatened and cornered, the hierarchy uses the process of excommunication to silence those seeking change and wields the threat of spiritual alienation from God to force people back to its orthodoxy. This "charter for protection," created by the clergy and dedicated to preserving their authority and positions, created an institutional system whose DNA imprints "survival at any cost" on those who run the organization.

If you have any doubt of this, consider the oath new cardinals take when they receive the red hat. At the last consistory in February 2012, twenty-two cardinals were appointed. As part of the ritual, each cardinal recited the traditional oath of loyalty, pledging to remain faithful to the Church and "not to make known to anyone matters entrusted to me in confidence, the disclosure of which could bring damage or dishonor to Holy Church." No wonder the children of abuse never had a chance for justice. Pope Benedict's request of his new cardinals was, "And pray for me, that I may continually offer to the People of God the witness of sound doctrine and guide the holy church with a firm and humble hand." He will use that firm hand to protect his power and the power of his bishops and priests, to ensure the People of God remain under his control. The clergy's commitment to secrecy and protection of the Church—not to the education, awareness, and involvement of the People of God—undermines the so-called commitment to transparency.

These strategies are effective due to a laity that has chosen to remain dependent and has allowed others to impede the psychological and spiritual development necessary to become fully human and fully Christian. Laypeople must educate themselves and find the confidence and authority to become "Christian Catholics," a phrase I will use throughout the book to describe our charter to embrace the message of the first word and to commit to reform the second.

This book is about breaking the hold the organizational Church has on the People of God who are the foundation of the Christian Catholic community. I am going to challenge the logic loop among three basic elements the Church uses to keep people dependent and spiritually indebted to the organization: the self-serving institutional interpretation of the gospel message, the theology that attempts to codify and control the gospel message, and the unilateral power system of the political Church organization. These three constitute a crucible of struggle for those attempting to break away and take responsibility for their spiritual lives.

Having worked in corporate life most of my career, I know how difficult it is for people to change, especially those who already have power and are asked to share it or give it up. That is why I have not directed this book to bishops and priests, because they have no organizational incentive to change. Some may have a sincere commitment to grow and challenge the status quo, but it doesn't translate to any sort of large-scale initiative to improve the organization. Even bishops and priests of goodwill who believe in the changes I'm going to suggest are trapped by the commitments they have made to the organizational Church and will be punished if they stray away from those commitments.

Unlocking Spiritual Handcuffs

This work invites laypeople to drive the change by assessing the current state of their relationship with the Church and by evaluating the past or current roadblocks that keep them from taking responsibility for their personal spirituality. With the support of others of like mind, individual Christian Catholics can accept the challenge and make the commitment to put into action the following levers for change:

- Grow to a level of spiritual maturity in which they can discern what is right for them and take responsibility for their choices, even if they contradict what the Church is espousing.

- Have the courage, psychologically and spiritually, to leave the Church and work out their independence from the organization. Then, and only then, they may choose to return and reform the systems and structure to ensure their ownership of the Catholic community on multiple levels, including economic.

- Eradicate the relationship of dependence they have on the Church and its ministers, and institute a spirit of partnership and mutual interdependence as the basis for dialogue and change among the members of a Christian Catholic community.

- Assert their right as baptized Christian Catholics, regardless of race, sexual orientation, or gender, to fulfill any role in the community they are qualified for and called to by the community.

Therefore, the intent of this book is to awaken in all Christian Catholics the relationship they have with the Church and to help them evaluate whether their commitment to Christianity is by informed choice or by the unexamined acceptance of a dependent relationship to a hierarchical institution. This material hopefully will inspire (breathe life into), all members of the Church who have felt frightened, abused, excluded, or injured. If it does, may it also awaken within them the desire to create an experience of the Church based on their participation as loving and valued members of a Christian Catholic community.

The process of understanding and assessing this participation will be framed by using the concepts of Authorship, Partnership, and Collaborative Organizations. These concepts will allow us to discern whether our thoughts, feelings, and actions are controlled by the policies and practices of the organizational Church or whether we are intellectually, emotionally, and behaviorally independent. Will that independence allow us to challenge the hierarchy to improve the community of believers and enhance the clerical and lay service to members of the Church? Will we move forward, even at the risk of alienation and censure, and utilize psychological, theological, spiritual, and economic levers in conjunction with other members of our Christian Catholic community to insist on reform? These questions will focus our discussion as we proceed.

The Goals of This Book

I hope this material will generate discussions that will lead to the achievement of the following goals:

- That a dialogue will be created among Christian Catholics that will result in them taking total responsibility for their lives and giving support to one another in their communities.

- That a renewal process will begin between laity and clergy whereby roles and responsibilities will be redefined and ownership of all assets of the community will be redistributed and managed based on competence and contribution rather than on power and position.

- That a fundamental discussion of the basics of good leadership, high-performance teams, and effective organizational systems will engage Christian Catholics to reorganize their communities based on partnership and collaborative organizations.

Progress toward achievement of these goals will help people to live free of fear and dependence and to accept responsibility along with others in their community for the growth and vitality of their Christian Catholic community.

What This Book Is Not

- The book does not delve into the theological issues around one's personal relationship and faith in God, Jesus, or "being saved." I'll leave that search to you, the reader, since it's a lifelong, evolving, nonlinear, challenging journey.

- It does not deal with scholarly interpretations of New Testament Scripture. However, it does offer explanations of key Scriptures that the Church has used to secure its unilateral authority.

- It's not a solution for people, but a diagnostic so they can challenge their beliefs and reevaluate their current relationship with the Church.

- This book is not about destroying the Catholic Church. Some of the hierarchy and clergy are doing a good job of that on their own.

Where We Go from Here

The book is divided into three sections. The first deals with the protection system of the Church and how the Church has used various aspects of the Gospels, theology, and its organizational power to control its members and maintain their allegiance. I also discuss the counterarguments to eliminate the control of the Church and encourage parishioners to accept total responsibility for their spiritual lives.

The second section explains the interrelated concepts of Authorship, Partnership, and Collaborative Organizations as the personal and institutional framework for reform. This section builds the foundations for self-reliance and inter-dependent mutual support toward developing a Christian Catholic community. The chapters on partnership and col-laborative organizations are more didactic, but try to slosh through them, because these two chapters are important for understanding how your sense of authorship is utilized in challenging the Church.

The third section outlines a path to reform driven by the laity. It lays out the resources necessary to ensure significant movement toward building a community that behaves as a beacon for those seeking the refuge of a Christian commu-nity. This doesn't mean the clergy are excluded from the re-form, but if they find a place in the movement, it may place them outside their commitment to the institution and their own comfort zone.

The book includes stories and examples of people who have influenced my life, some explanations of core concepts necessary for understanding my conclusions, and a bit of hu-mor to lighten the seriousness of the discussion. Through-out the book, you will see the letters NB in bold, followed by declarative statements. The little Latin I retain asks that you *nota bene* (note well) these statements, because they are critical to understanding or accepting a process or issue. For example, **NB:** When I use the term Church, I am referring to the institution. I will use the term People of God when I am referring to lay Church members. Bishops and priests will be considered as clergy or hierarchy and as part of the institutional system.

Bridging the Gap

In a recent interview, Neil deGrasse Tyson, the eminent astrophysicist, spoke of the necessity at times to reach out into the abyss between what is known and what is unknown—to make something up that might be true so you can organize a research plan to create a bridge to discover the truth. Similarly, our intent is to explore and create a bridge of discovery, the planks of which will be laid by the knowledge of, acceptance of, and total responsibility for our lives. We are going to "make up" an alternative to the status quo, through which we will consider the possibilities whereby the organizational Church will either get out of the way or evolve to the maturity necessary to serve the People of God. We are going to create a new approach to a Catholic Church community that is untested and will need to evolve based on the wisdom of the people.

If you are intrigued by what is written in these pages, consider exploring works by other writers on the interpretations I make and the conclusions I draw. At the end of each section are recommendations for follow-up reading that will give a more comprehensive overview of how I developed my conclusions.

Life Is Change; Growth Is Optional

This book describes a journey I have made over the last forty-five years. I don't have solutions for other people's lives. I have only my story as a flawed human being who grew in his awareness of his need to change and grow in the roles of priest, husband, businessman, and friend. I have met countless people who have described their injury by the Church as irreconcilable or who feel stuck by the rigidity of its doctrine and its irrelevance to real-life problems. In dealing with my own injury as a child and later as a priest in the Catholic Church, I found a way to move away and gain the perspective that has allowed me the freedom to tell my story so that it might benefit others. In so doing, my wounds are healed, and the scars are a reminder never to allow anyone to take away my responsibility for the problems and choices that are necessary for my growth.

After devoting years to helping others, Carl Jung made a striking observation as to how people are and are not healed:

"All the greatest and most important problems of life are fundamentally insoluble...They can never be solved but only outgrown. This "outgrowing" proved on further investigation to require a new level of *consciousness*. Some higher or wider interest appeared on the patient's horizon, and through this broadening of his or her outlook the insoluble problem lost its urgency. It was not solved logically in its own terms, but faded when confronted with a new and stronger life urge." [1]

Hopefully, the time you invest in this book will bring you to a new level of consciousness that will lead to new possibilities. Those possibilities will provide opportunities for new choices and new actions that can result in you having a different relationship with the Church.

Now you will need to summon equal parts curiosity and courage to turn the page. The journey in this book is not primarily about changing the Catholic Church. It is about your internal change that allows for a mature, interdependent relationship with the Church. When that happens among a critical mass of people who desire reform and who have the knowledge and skills to drive effective strategies, then the organization will change.

The potentially frightening part of this discovery is that you won't need the organizational Church. You may come to that realization before you discover what you do need and from whom. If you maintain a strong curiosity and a healthy skepticism, you will get there—wherever "there" is for you. You will change if you read on. What that change will be and where it leads you is the adventure to be experienced in these pages.

Let's begin.

CHAPTER 1

CHANGING FROM
THE INSIDE OUT

*I want to throw open the windows of the Church so that we
can see out and the people can see in.*
— Pope John XXIII

Interestingly, it was a dark and stormy night when I was
called to the front office of the rectory to meet a couple with
a serious family issue. The weather and the conversation are
etched in my memory because the story I listened to was a perfect storm—a damned if you do, damned if you don't scenario.
Briefly, they were a couple in their early thirties with four children and had been struggling with the guilt of using contraception to prevent more pregnancies. The Church's position is
that if a couple uses contraception, they are not permitted to
go to communion or receive absolution, even if they confess
but aren't willing to stop using birth control. The fact is, they
were going to communion, but felt very guilty that they might
be committing a greater sin.

I'll tell you the rest of the story and the decision they
made to break out of their dilemma, but first we have to discuss some ideas and terms that are integral to their eventual
choices.

Gospel Interpretation

In its broadest yet most direct explanation, the Gospels of the New Testament are an invitation to explore love of self, love of neighbor, and love of God; forgiveness of self, forgiveness of neighbor, and forgiveness by God. I don't mean it as a linear progression, but an evolutionary, interactive awakening over time beginning with love and forgiveness of self that deepens with an awakening relationship with God. However, this gospel message has been interpreted and distorted at times by Church scholars who developed theological and political systems that favor protection of the organizational Church over service to the People of God.

Theological Doctrine

Due to a host of issues, ranging from multiple gospel accounts and interpretations as to who Jesus was, as well as a variety of heresies and schisms, a systemic approach to thinking about God, Jesus, and humanity's relationship to them developed. This approach is called theology, which is the rational and systematic study of God. Over the centuries, Catholic theologians had immense influence on the Church's teachings. Doctors of the Church, such as Augustine and Thomas Aquinas, developed doctrines that were affirmed as "truths" by councils such as Nicaea and Trent, and enforced throughout history by a Roman curia that used censure, excommunication, and even death to quell the voices of opposition.

Theological study has been the domain of clerical and lay scholars whose conclusions have set the foundation and logical framework for understanding the "Jesus of history and the Christ of faith" themes interwoven in the gospels. Although old scholarship justifies the primacy of the clergy and of the organizational system of rules and regulations to control the beliefs and actions of the people, new insights from other scholars such as the Swiss Catholic theologian Hans Kung assign a significant role to the wisdom of the People of God in the evolution of spirituality, and of the Church community.

Organizational Systems of Control

The Church's structure, systems, power, and authority provide the organizational lens through which it sees not only itself and the roles of its hierarchy and members but also its relationship to the rest of the world. Its charter is based on certain passages of Scripture that mistakenly allowed clergy unilateral authority over all things temporal and spiritual; an authority that is reinforced by a long tradition of circular logic that ensures its longevity.

Three components—gospel interpretation, a theological doctrine of certainty, and organizational control—form the protective system of the organizational Church we spoke of in the preface. It's structured as a three-legged stool comprised of the New Testament text interpreted by Catholic scholars, Catholic theology created by Catholic scholars, and the tradition of the organizational Church compiled by Catholic scholars and perpetuated by the Catholic hierarchy and clergy. Do we see a trend here?

Once this system is under attack or forced into a defensive position, it has three ways to protect itself from the threat. The first is *control*, which tries to reinforce the need for certainty and to use the fear of punishment after death to bring people in line. The second is to force *compliance* through punishment such as withdrawing membership or access to sacraments or community involvement. The third is *indifference*, the passive-aggressive approach that responds with apparent agreement and then does nothing.

The process of managing your life from a stance of protection places you in a precarious loop that is difficult to break. The circular process goes something like this: When you have been trained as a Catholic and react to a problem or moral issue out of a sense of protection, your first response is usually "What does the Church say?" If you use the Church as one resource while exploring other resources, it may be effective as long as you retain ultimate authority and responsibility to make the decision. But, if you give the problem solving and decision making to someone else, and you don't rely on your own authority to resolve the threat or issue, you depend on that person or institution for the solution. When you do that, you allow the other to tell you what to do. Your need for certainty causes you to place the ownership for the problem in someone else's hands. It also transfers to someone else the ownership and development of solutions for the problem. So now you must rely on the other resource, who is providing a solution that may or may not work—and that creates dependency. Dependency, especially in adults, can create anger, and the basis of anger is fear. The ineffective management of fear calls for protection, and the loop is closed.

Want another ticket for that merry-go-round? If Church leadership seeks to protect itself rather than to evolve and learn how to better serve its members, the same negative loop ensues. When the Church feels a need for protection because of a perceived external threat or problem, it develops approaches that affirm dogmatic certainty about the issue and responds to the perceived threat by using control, compliance, or indifference that we mentioned earlier. All three strategies can be very aggressive, depending on the choice of behaviors, which spans the gamut from physical attack to alienation and isolation.

The three-legged stool is constructed so that no matter where you start in the system, you can find a way to have the other two legs support your issue. For example, let's go back to the couple who can't afford more children and who can't use contraception, according to Church law. If they challenge the Church and ask for an explanation, since there is nothing in Scripture on this issue, here's how it will be handled from a theological or dogmatic approach:

Scripture Interpretation

At least two Scripture passages support the logic loop we spoke of earlier:

"All authority in heaven and earth has been given to me." (Matthew 28:18)

"Thou are Peter and upon this rock I will build my church.....Whatever you bind on earth will be considered bound in heaven; whatever you loose on earth will be considered loosed in heaven." (Matthew 16: 18-20)

So here's the logic: we, the hierarchical Church, have the authority to decide this issue because we have the power from Jesus to decide everything.

We will explore these passages more completely when we get to the concept of authorship in a later chapter, but let me leave you with this question for now: do you think Jesus intended to give total power to a group of men when he spent much of his public ministry decrying the misuse of positional authority by the Priests and Pharisees? I believe, along with many Scripture scholars, that the authors of the Gospels, as well as the editors who revised those documents through-out the first three centuries, attributed words to Jesus that he didn't speak. They were inserted to secure strong control over the Jewish converts and the rigid religious culture they were breaking from, as well as over non-Jewish converts who were breaking from belief in multiple gods. There is ample evidence in the Gospels that Jesus wanted men and women to grow as human beings by searching, exploring, and learning about themselves and their relationship with God. It was not Jesus's intent that people be told what is true by men who benefit from the relational and spiritual dependency of their parishioners. Just think about it for now.

Theology

Continuing further with this logic, the organizational Church can say, "Since we have the power, we can make the rules and determine the intention of God through Jesus concerning how life issues are to be handled." The obvious problem with this stance is that the Church leaders are inconsistent in their application. For example, the Church contends all life is sacred and must have a chance to evolve. That is why it condemns abortion, suicide, assisted suicide, contraception, stem cell research, and so on. Yet war is often rationalized and the Inquisition, Crusades, persecution of the Jews, and forced conversions of native peoples were all initiated or encouraged by the Church hierarchy of the time. Finally, how can you say you honor life when you allow children to be abused while protecting the perpetrators with silence, cover-up, and payoffs?

Organizational Control

The organization proclaims and requires you to adhere to its interpretation of the gospel and its theological rationale for you to be a member in good standing. So, if you don't buy the first two elements of its logic, you can't belong to the Catholic Community. Point, match, game over.

However, any good priest will tell you that the ultimate decision maker for moral choices is the individual with an informed conscience. Developing an informed conscience requires an open mind and heart, a significant amount of self-reflection, and a commitment to look at the issue or problem from different viewpoints. So, if another child is going to strain the parental ability financially to raise, educate, house, feed, and clothe other children, or risk the physical and psychological relationship with a spouse, then who is best qualified to make a decision about another pregnancy? The Church says the parents own the problem, but the solution as to what they can do with the problem remains with the Church. Checkmate! However, we will break this logic when we present the new three-legged stool that is the basis of transition from Catholic orthodoxy to Christian responsibility.

Celibacy is another example of this logic loop. There is nothing in Scripture about the mandate that clergy must be celibate. Celibacy is a fifth-century rule enacted by the organization and justified by an interpretation of the Gospels that says Jesus didn't marry, so priests shouldn't marry. Priests can then better imitate the life of Christ and give all to preaching the gospel and serving their parishioners. Celibacy isn't an essential part of priesthood, and may be, for some priests, an impediment to their psychological and spiritual development.

If you look at traditions within and outside the Roman Catholic tradition, you can see many examples of married clergy. The Diocese of Sacramento has admitted a Lutheran minister to the Catholic clergy with his wife standing by his side. Celibacy for the organizational Church is a social and economic threat, which is why it has been indifferent to the calls for change. I can't imagine a bishop trying to tell my wife how to behave because her husband is a priest. But, for pure entertainment value, I would buy a ticket to that confrontation.

Even when the Gospels clearly state a moral stance concerning children, the Church hierarchy went against it in favor of the organization's reputation. Look at how many bishops handled the threat of the abuse scandal. Until they were forced to accountability, all of their actions were designed to protect the Church and its clerical system. They used their power by issuing an injunction of silence to prevent and control the flow of information to the members, who would have been enraged by their duplicity. The Bishops crafted a message of defense that said, in essence, "We will handle the problem, but we won't speak about it openly." The hierarchy made the problem *un*discussable and paid off or threatened those who wanted to expose the issue. Even the attempt to discuss the *un*discussable was ignored. Can you imagine the fear and subsequent guilt parents of abused children were feeling when they were paid off for their silence to protect the Church's reputation?

The abuse scandal finally became known primarily because Christian Catholics had the courage to say, "We *will* discuss the abuse of children. We *will not* listen to your injunctions. We *will not* be silenced by your money or punishments. We *will* be heard." They had to go to the press and use the justice system to bring the malfeasance to light. The good news from this process is that it showed that the people can change the Church and require reform and accountability from those who have failed in their stewardship. Effective management of this issue by the hierarchy at the outset would have involved courage, transparency, education, and intervention, and would have saved countless children and their families from significant trauma. None of these qualities was evident in the bishops of this country, let alone in those bishops of so-called Catholic countries such as Ireland.

The Church also protects itself from discussing with candor and openness its exclusion of women and gay people from priesthood. Consider the Church's position in response to a woman or gay person who feels called to serve as a priest, and see if it makes any sense to you considering our discussion thus far. If we believe in "the call to service," then we know, according to research done by Father Donald Cozzens and others that between twenty-five to fifty percent of men who are gay have already been called to serve as priests.[1] The key reason women haven't been admitted is that they can't hide their gender, but I believe their vocation, "their call," is there waiting for the hierarchy to get out of the way.

NB: Challenging the Loop

The only way out of the loop is to regain the personal authority that the Church has taken by challenging the belief that the laity are dependent on the Church. We will explore the loop-breaking process when we discuss you as author and co-creator of life. Until then, sit with this thought: you don't need protection from the Church, and the Church doesn't need protection from you. The Church can't take your problems away from you, and you can't be effective as a choice-making human being if you try to give your problems to the Church and defer to its solutions. All relationships based on protection, fear, and the exercise of unilateral authority by one party over the other are doomed to failure.

Now, back to our courageous couple. The decision they made took several conversations, with significant input from each of us. We entered a partnership to resolve the issue, and although I'm not proud of some of the counsel I gave, the constructs we put in place and the final solution we came up with were the best we could develop at the time. Back then, in 1970, I was twenty-six, overeducated in irrelevant knowledge, unmarried, earning 175 dollars a month plus room and board, so I didn't have a lot of wisdom concerning people living in the real world.

The couple decided to continue on birth control and to continue to go to communion. They also agreed not to confess this as a sin and to check in periodically with each other and with me to see if they were still at peace with their decision.

However, they had difficulty not confessing "the sin," so we got creative. The second construct we put in place allowed them to admit to something they were not but believed they were. They said they felt like sinners because of the Church's stance on birth control and needed forgiveness before they could go to communion. I asked about their belief in communion, and their response came right out of the Catechism: it was the presence of Jesus. I then asked what one of Jesus's missions was, and they responded, "To save sinners."

My logic to them was, "If you believe Jesus is present in communion, and you believe you are sinners, you need to go to communion to be in his presence." (See Matthew 9:13; Mark 2:17.)

"But don't we have to confess first?" they asked. Unfortunately, I told them to confess only to me, and that left them in a dependent relationship, which fortunately didn't last

10

long. With continued conversations, they came to see that the responsibility, authority, and power to choose what was best for their family rested within them. They continued to receive communion, and no new children entered the scene.

As you can imagine, when my logic leaked out to their friends and my office visits began to increase, my pastor and bishop made it very clear that they didn't want me doing any more Scripture interpretations or dogma rewriting. Being a child of the sixties, I promptly ignored them, since I was ordained primarily to share the good news with the People of God, not to support organizational policies inconsistent with the gospel. From what I can gather from many priests today, most Catholics don't listen to the Church on birth control issues anymore. Any priest that counsels those struggling with a moral issue not to receive communion is serving Church regulation and not the gospel message. Can I hear an amen?

The trust this couple eventually put in themselves and in their own authority was born out of a necessity to solve a problem that threatened their relationship psychologically, physically, spiritually, and economically. The transformational process required a shift in the belief of who was responsible for the problem and whose authority they were going to listen to. This shift enabled them to choose love over fear and guilt.

The next chapters describe the components of that journey, which shifted not only my whole pastoral approach for the rest of my ministry but also my subsequent personal and professional life. Take your time going through these next chapters; the content can be challenging but will provide the basis for a new awareness of self and how you came "to be."

Take a minute and read the reflections carefully. Pay special attention to your resistance as you read and see if you can determine the source of the resistance.

Reflections

☑ Catholics belong to a church system that is self-protected, and requires, if they are to remain in good standing, acceptance of interpretations, doctrinal certainties, and organizational compliance that breed dependency.

☑ This dependency takes problem ownership away from its members and requires minimal discernment of or responsibility for life's moral and spiritual issues.

☑ The Church hierarchy and organizational systems react to threat and conflict with control, compliance, or indifference.

☑ Many theological doctrines were developed to maintain the laity's dependency by threatening exclusion from the community and by promising afterlife rewards and punishments.

☑ Recognition and acceptance of personal responsibility and authority are more important than Church authority in resolving problems you own.

So, what's the strategy to break out of this loop? It involves a shift in thinking that allows movement from the concept of original sin to one of original blessing, from problem deflection to problem ownership, and from confessional dependency to forgiveness of self and others. Let's move forward.

Expanding Your Knowledge

Read *Misquoting* Jesus: *The story behind who changed the Bible and why*. Bart Ehrman, is the James A. Gray Distinguished Professor at the University of North Carolina at Chapel Hill. He describes the problems of interpreting Scripture and the role that politics played within both the Church and society on New Testament interpretation. [2]

In addition, consider James Carroll's book *Constantine's Sword: The Church and the Jews*. His book clearly shows the role the organizational Church has played over time in the discrimination against and persecution of the Jews as well as providing a great history of the early Church [3]

CHAPTER 2

THINKING
OUTSIDE THE NINE DOTS

*We can't solve problems by using the same kind of thinking we
used when we created them.*
— A. EINSTEIN

Anyone who has spent time in corporate life or attended a course on creativity had been challenged with the following problem:

Put nine dots on a piece of paper in the following configuration:

Now, without removing your pen from the paper, connect all nine dots with four straight lines. When you change the direction of the first line, you begin the second line and so forth. (I'll put the solution at the end of the chapter to keep your frustration to a minimum.) Most people try to solve the problem by keeping the lines inside the parameters of the nine dots. But the way to solve it is to draw the lines outside the dots. And that's what I suggest you do as you look at your relationship with the Church: look outside the current structure and dogma of the Church so you can research and assess material that will help you reengage the Church as a powerful, confident Christian Catholic.

Childhood beliefs—what we have been taught and what we still think or feel is true—drive the dependency we have on the Church. The core spiritual belief is that we are born into original sin and must be baptized in the Church to be freed from that sin. We then seek forgiveness for our sins from the ministers of the Church for the rest of our lives. The underlying belief is that we don't have to own responsibility for our problems or to seek forgiveness from those we have injured to "get right with God." Why? Because Saturday-night confession is right around the corner, and we receive forgiveness from a priest whether we have sought forgiveness from those we have wronged or injured—be they spouse, children, or neighbor.

As I mentioned earlier, a three-legged stool supports the Church's protection system. I suggest a different approach by offering a three-legged stool made up of original blessing, problem ownership, and personal reconciliation. This approach will challenge the relevance of the Church's three-legged stool of protection provided by a self-serving Gospel interpretation, theological doctrine of certainty, and organizational control.

Original Blessing

The first shift we need to make is from the concepts of the theology of the fall and redemption to the theology of God creating with the intention of original blessing. The conviction that you come in to the world as an original blessing, free of sin, rather than as a child with original sin, becomes your first turning point toward a new belief about your relationship with God and acceptance of yourself. The question is, are you open to this change in belief that sees yourself as unconditionally lovable and valuable? If so, are you also open to consider the impact this new view of yourself will have on your thinking, feeling, speaking, and doing in relation to the Church? Let's see if I can help you make the turn.

Because of Augustine and the Council of Trent, the concept of original sin became the pivotal doctrine through which the Church has maintained control over its members. But recent scholarship has suggested that Augustine got it wrong and that Trent was controlled by political circumstances as well as by the intent to provide theological clarity. I refer you to "Path 1, Theme 2" in Matthew Fox's book *Original Blessing*. [1] He concludes that there is no basis in Scripture for the concept of original sin:

- The concept was developed based on a mistranslation by Augustine.

- The Council of Trent never defined what original sin was.

- Jewish scholars had the "Book" a thousand years before Christians did, and they never saw the Garden story as the basis for original sin.

In his work, *Is Original Sin in Scripture?*, Herbert Haag, former president of the Catholic Bible Association of Germany, wrote: "The doctrine of original sin is not found in any of the writings of the Old Testament. It is certainly not in chapters 1 through 3 of Genesis. This ought to be recognized today not only by Old Testament Scholars but by dogmatic theologians."[2]

He further states, "No man, (or woman), enters the world a sinner. As the creature and image of God, he is from his first hour surrounded by God's Fatherly love. Consequently, he is not at birth,...an enemy of God and a child of God's wrath. A man becomes a sinner only through his own individual and responsible action."[3]

Finally, Matthew Fox wrote, "We enter a broken and torn and sinful world—that is for sure. But we do not enter as blotches on existence, as sinful creatures; we burst in to the world as "original blessings". And anyone who has joyfully brought children in to the world knows this."[4]

I think it's reasonable to assume from Genesis that the metaphorical Adam came into the world as an original blessing. God didn't put him on the Earth with the challenge to find the way back as a function of an undefined sin that gets passed down to future generations because of an undefined harm to the relationship with God. The human construct that saddles a son or daughter with a debt owed to the father is a projection onto God that allows the Church to justify its role as mediator and judge, requiring dependency from its members. It isn't rational or possible for children to come into the world alienated from the God who breathed life into their very existence. As the kids say, "Let's get real!"

In his book, *On Being a Christian*, Hans Kung asserts, "Jesus did not proclaim any theological theory or any new law, nor did he proclaim himself. He proclaimed the kingdom of God: God's cause=God's will, which will prevail and which is identical with man's cause=man's well-being." [5]

If you buy God's will and humankind's well-being as the intention of a loving God, you can't have that same loving God putting a "spiritual clamp" on children coming into this world. Doctrine should not preclude common sense, especially when it attempts to lower God to the level of our petty human failings. Doesn't it seem more reasonable that a loving God would provide the same blessing to all who enter the world?

So why is it in the best interest of the Church to keep the fall/redemption theology in place? Let's take a quick look at the concept of sin first and then at the Church's intrusion into the process of reconciliation.

What is sin? The Greek root of the word means, "missing the target." It's a behavior that's inconsistent with the intended goal or target. As we mentioned before, the general goal is humankind's well-being as a fulfillment of God's will. When we act in a way that's inconsistent with our well-being or that of another, sin is possible. If you look through the fall/redemption lens of theology, you see yourself coming into the world alienated from God and needing salvation. The creation-centered concept of sin looks at life as dualistic and sees relationships in terms of subject/object with the result that you experience separation from all the things and people you encounter.

Matthew Fox made this clear in *Original Blessing*: "Take any sin; war, burglary, rape, thievery. Every such action is treating another as an object outside oneself. This is dualism. This is behind all sin." He further stated his case by quoting Mahatma Gandhi, who believed that "the basic sin and the only sin is separateness. He who conquers this sin conquers all others." [6]

When we discuss forgiveness, we will see that the first step in the process is the recognition that we are connected to the one injured. When we see no connection to the other—man, woman, child, or nature itself—then unspeakable sin is possible. As Jacques Cousteau was fond of saying about our relationship to all creatures, "We may be different but we are not distinct."

The Church needs members to be dependent on its system for dealing with sin. Here is the logic:

- The Church sees you as someone enmeshed in original sin and the fall/redemption cycle of theology when you were born. This becomes, as marketers would say, "their demographic," which pretty much includes all of humanity.

- If you come into the world needing redemption because you are already a sinner, and the Church has set up the system to convince you it has the power and means to remove the sin, you come into the world dependent on the Church and its process to remove sin. Therefore, when members sin, they are dependent on Church ministers for an interpretation of the severity of their wrongdoing and for reconciliation through confession and absolution. That's the logic loop that ensures dependency and creates the spiritual merry-go-round.

NB: Make this affirmation daily for a week, and see if your previous perceptions change:

At my birth, I was an original blessing. I was a creation brought in to the world blameless and at that moment was filled with love and grace. The rest—the good, the bad, and the ugly—I learned later.

If you can wrap your head and heart around the fact that you started off as a gift to life and that your value is guaranteed, you need to deal only with your learned internal beliefs and unacceptable behavior as a cause of the separateness in your relationships with others. You are of unconditional value. It's your behavior that may need correction, and that begins with you owning the problems generated in your life.

Problem Ownership

Who owns the problem? I can't tell you the number of times I've used that question as I've worked with corporations to resolve customer issues or deal with manufacturing defects. It's one of the essential questions to ask in resolving any problem or conflict in the business world. That question is also critical when we're dealing with relationships, especially when the power and responsibilities of those in the relationship are unequal and one party is dependent on the other.

The concept of problem ownership is simple in its logic, difficult in its discipline, and profound in its impact on your freedom. It's the one idea you must understand if you are to take back your responsibility as a Christian Catholic. Problem ownership was part of a model of communication and interpersonal problem solving that I learned while attending a class on effective communication. The instructor began by asking, "How do you know someone has a problem?" With his help, we created the following list:

- A person tells you they have a problem. Simple, elegant, and rarely done.

- Affect change: The person exhibits nonverbal behaviors of anger, sadness, fear, and so on. Most spouses can tell when something is amiss with their partner without a word being spoken. This is especially true of parents with children.

- Coded message: A person has a presenting problem that's not the real issue. For example, when your child comes home from school and says, "I hate school," you usually suspect a specific incident rather than the school being all bad.

- Signal behavior: Lying, cheating, and stealing are indicators of a problem in children as well as in adults. Add the modern-day issues of drug abuse, self-mutilation, anorexia, and so on, and the alarms should be going off for the individual as well as for those around him or her.

- Fight, flight, or withdrawal: This is the trifecta of responses to conflict, any of which indicates clearly that someone has a problem.

After finishing the list and exhausting the parental and spousal stories about "them" having a problem, the instructor asked a follow-up question: "We agree that when we see the above behaviors, both verbal and nonverbal, in the other person, it's a clear indication they have a problem, right?"

We all said, "Yes," and I could feel my gut tighten as the next words came out of his mouth.

"So, when you see the above behaviors, both verbal and nonverbal, in yourself, it means you have a problem, and the only question left is whether you are going to own it or blame someone else for it."

That set off a round of examples from the group of why he was wrong, beginning with the phrase, "Yes, but…"

The instructor listened patiently and said, "If you don't own the problem, how can you be involved in and own the search for a solution to your problem?"

The discussion went on for some time, but I retreated into my head and heart, and jotted down some concepts that keep me grounded today:

- Problem ownership ultimately means no blame. The extent to which I blame is the extent to which I keep the problem and therefore the possibility of a good solution away from myself.

- If I blame others for what is rightly my problem, I also give them tremendous power in determining whether the problem will be solved.

- When I blame others, I expect *them* to change so my life will work again. However, fulfilling your expectation may be impeded by the other person.

  - ∞ The other doesn't want to change.
  - ∞ I create expectations about what he or she "should" and "ought" to do to make my life work, when that person might not know or care about my expectations.
  - ∞ The other person isn't aware she or he is causing me a problem so she or he sees no need to change.
  - ∞ The person knows I want him or her to change, and in not changing, he or she continues to control the drama. (Anyone with teenagers knows this one well.)

∞ If I blame others for the problem, the solution rests with them. They can choose to provide a solution that:
* doesn't work for me;
* works for me, but keeps me dependent in the relationship;
* keeps my life on hold until they decide to offer a solution.

• When I take a problem away from others, even with the best intentions, I rob them of the opportunity to enhance their problem-solving skills and to take credit for a solution that has improved their life. I can consult, facilitate, and educate, but I can't take away their problem without consequences to their sense of worth and competence. Why? Because the fundamental building blocks of self-worth are a sense of unconditional lovability and the competence to resolve problems.

This list is not exhaustive, so take a moment to think about your own experience when someone has taken a problem from you. What did you think and feel when that happened? Now walk in the shoes of someone you took a problem from, and think about the effect on him or her. The message is, "I don't think you have the self-worth, confidence, or competence to solve the problem." If you want to help someone with a problem, use the skills of education, facilitation, or consultation—don't impose your solution.

Reflect on and integrate the following as part of your problem-ownership assessment. This is an **NB** moment, so take your time to understand these points:

☑ What you think and feel, say and do belongs to you; you own the behavior. As an adult, no one can make you think, feel, or do anything unless you allow it. "

☑ If you want to give up power, blame others. If you want to lose creativity in resolving the issues of your life, blame others.

☑ Your *reaction* to what others say and do is *information about you* for you to assess. Your reaction informs you about what you are thinking and feeling, and that is yours to own.

☑ Their *reaction* to what you say and do is *information about them* for you to assess. Their reaction to *you* is what they are thinking and feeling and is theirs to own. However, their reaction to you might sometimes inform you about possible changes in your behavior or attitudes that you need to consider to enhance the relationship.

NB: The last two checked boxes are very important in understanding who owns the problem and how to sort out relationship responsibility. Take your time with these concepts. However, be clear that you can't figure out whether you are lovable or not. It's not an issue of proof, but an issue of acceptance. If you don't accept your value as a loving human being, you will justify all harm you do to others and defend against the harm they do to you. Your intrinsic value is a condition of your existence and is a perpetual state that requires you need only to remember to bring it to consciousness. Unfortunately, the injury done to us when we are children can make it difficult for us to accept our value as adults.

Personal Reconciliation: Forgiveness in a Box

So, now you know you are of value and you own your own problems, but unfortunately you aren't perfect. Therefore, when your behavior is unacceptable and harms you or another, it's time to consider a process of forgiveness.

In the late sixties, people went to confession in a structure called the "box." It consisted of three wooden sections. The priest sat in the middle, separated by a wall with a small cutout covered by a screen. The penitents were on either side, kneeling and waiting for the priest to slide back the screen and begin listening. Just the image of people kneeling gives you a sense of the power inequality and dependent nature of the experience. When I was "in the box" for Saturday confessions, most of the things I heard were minor issues generated primarily by a lack of maturity and ineffective communication skills. A simple statement of the "sin," plus two Our Fathers and Three Hail Marys took care of the issue. "In and out in five," as we used to say.

This type of confession was simple and quick, and it masked a very dependent relationship that prevented real psychological and spiritual pain from surfacing and being resolved. I generally listened to many "sins" that came from early learning and parental mistakes, generated in the "soup" we call our family of origin. None of us was raised in a perfect household with perfect parents, and since this isn't a book on psychology or an explanation of the social impact of poor potty training, I'm leaving that discussion for you to research if you're interested.

When I started to challenge the "in and out in five," my lines for Saturday confession began to get shorter; men especially began to avoid my box. I started to ask them to think about what was going on when they yelled at their spouse or children, or came home drunk and abusive. The response was usually "I don't know." The question surprised them, and not wanting to let them off the hook, I said, "Take a guess." This led to either silence or throwaway lines like "I was in a bad place."

Given the time constraints and the fact that the penitent in those days was kneeling, I told them their penance was to go home and find the reason they hurt the other person—and they couldn't start the explanation with "They made me..." When they figured it out as best they could, they could then apologize to the one they injured. The immediate response was, "Where are the two Our Fathers and three Hail Marys?" They wanted to walk away feeling right with God and the Church, but they didn't want to put effort into healing the injured relationship. The confessional was a construct of dependency that allowed people to skate through the consequences of their behavior without any pressure from the priest to get them to face their issues. This was not effective for immature people who habitually injured themselves or others.

When my pastor heard about the unique penances that were being given out, especially to his golfing buddies, I was reminded that I was not a psychologist and shouldn't be delving into the motivations of others. I think his real concern was how much more work he had to do on Saturday, since people were going to his confessional box and avoiding mine.

Just before I left active ministry, my response to people in confession was very different from when I started. As I reflect back, the movement for me went from a focus on the sin and a "two and three" penance to looking at the goodness of people as the source for their change; giving support to them so they could own the problem; and encouraging them to select their own penance. It was all I knew at the time to break the dependency—and this brings us to a discussion of the final leg of the stool.

Acknowledge the Power to Heal Your Life

"Confession is good for the soul" as the saying goes, but why, and for whom? Since I was a priest and priests are involved in forgiving others, I asked myself why I had to go to another priest when I needed forgiveness. I could have said, "Pat, you have recognized the mistake and asked forgiveness from the one injured; you are now forgiven by the Father Pat side of yourself." I agree it's a shaky construct, but one that started me thinking about the process of confession and reconciliation, and why I had the concept right but for all the wrong reasons.

The Catholic process of confession breeds dependence on the organization. Confession in its basic form requires a priest who has the organizational power to provide forgiveness or withhold it, and the power to give penance. It requires only that the penitent tell the sin, intend to change, and do the penance—and they are good to go. Unless the priest is aware and behaves in a way that helps the penitent take responsibility for personal reconciliation, the confession maintains the status quo, which is ultimately ineffective.

There is a Scripture that commands personal reconciliation between you and God as well as between you and your neighbor that doesn't require an intermediary: "But when the Pharisees heard that he had silenced the Sadducees, they gathered together. And one of them, a lawyer, asked him a question to test him. Teacher, which is the great commandment in the Law? And he said to him, you should love the Lord your God with all your heart and with all your soul and with your entire mind. This is the great and first commandment. And a second is like it: You shall love your neighbor as yourself" (Matthew 22: 34-39).

Since the development of any relationship requires love, and the sustaining of that relationship requires forgiveness, it follows that the power to love and forgive lives in each of us. A third party may be helpful to educate, council, and encourage—not to judge and impose punishment. Just add the word *forgiveness* to the second commandment and see how that places the power to love and forgive yourself and others right in the palm of your hand. "You shall forgive your neighbor as yourself".

The Church has kept the understanding and process of forgiveness narrowly defined within the dependent framework of the confessional. If its ministers supported Matthew 22, they would be teaching the psychology of self-worth and effective communication skills associated with a process of personal reconciliation.

The Latin phrase *nemo dat quod non habit* loosely translates as "You cannot give what you do not have." One application of that aphorism is that unless you forgive yourself first for an injury to another, you can't extend that forgiveness experience to the one injured. If there is no sense of wrongdoing, the expression of sorrow to the other is likely motivated by a fear of losing the relationship or by a manipulative desire to minimize the tension and get things back to "normal" or to an uneasy truce. It's essential to love and forgive yourself before you can give that forgiveness to another with any genuineness.

The Five Components of Forgiveness

There are five components of personal reconciliation, and all must be included to experience true forgiveness, first of yourself and then of others. It's not essential for the other to respond or reciprocate for you to experience reconciliation within yourself. It's very helpful but not essential. I've listened to people grieving the loss of a parent or relative and feeling guilty about a past injury or harsh word for which they had not asked forgiveness. By engaging in a reconciliation process, they were able to find some peace in forgiving themselves and, based on the positive elements of the relationship, trust that the other would have reciprocated.

1. *Recognition* of the value of all involved in the harmful experience by acknowledging three elements of healthy relationships:

    a. Valuing yourself and the other. If you don't value yourself, you won't see yourself as worthy of forgiveness. If you don't value the other, you won't see him or her as deserving of forgiveness.

    b. Willingness to improve the relationship or to leave the relationship without rancor or guilt. Feelings of anger or guilt indicate unfinished business and a failure to let go of the injury or ongoing harm in the relationship.

    c. Openness to changing your behavior. If you want or expect the other person to change, be prepared for disappointment. Remember, you can own only your thoughts, feelings, and actions. You have no control over another. Forgiveness is based on what you think and feel, say and do, and is not contingent on the actions of the other.

2. *Responsibility.* Ownership of the behavior—without blame—that caused the injury or harm is the beginning of accepting responsibility for the experience and the first step toward possible solutions.

3. *Remorse.* Regret for the behavior and the harm caused. There are times when we justify our actions or blame the other for our response. Without a sense of regret, the process stops here, and you will carry the rationalization for your behavior with you.

4. *Restoration.* Appropriate response to mitigate the harm. You only need to offer to restore what was lost or harmed by your actions. It's not essential that the other accept it. The consequences and ownership for not accepting your forgiveness is now a problem for the other person.

5. *Resolution to stop.* Commitment and plan to cease the behavior. Habitual unacceptable behavior that causes harm to you or another usually needs professional help. If you find yourself saying, "I'm sorry" for the same behavior repeatedly, check out the cause and put a plan in place to change the behavior and mitigate the harm.

This five-step process is an audit to assess your readiness to seek, receive, and extend forgiveness. The more you reflect on the process, the more sense it will make, and it will free you from dependency on others. If you seek help from a priest, therapist, or friend, make sure that person provides only education or consultation, not an intervention that takes the issue from your responsibility.

Reflect on these key points:

Asking for forgiveness. If you seek forgiveness, request it without any ifs, ands, or buts that might lessen your sincere intention. For example, I have heard spouses ask for forgiveness by saying, "I am really sorry, but if only you would quit..." That style of asking for forgiveness usually starts the argument again. If the other party isn't willing to enter the process, the forgiveness of self and the love extended to the other is all that's necessary to bless the other, who can't or won't reciprocate at that moment.

Receiving forgiveness. When receiving forgiveness, accept it unconditionally, and that means not questioning the intention of the other. If the injury dictates a change in the relationship due to repeated, unacceptable behaviors, that's a problem to solve later.

Giving forgiveness. Do your own work first to determine your role in the harm, if any. When you give forgiveness, make sure you honor your value and that of the other. Don't judge the value of the person; only deal with the behavior at the moment you experienced the hurt. Jesus was very clear on the process that psychologists now call projection:

> "Do not judge, or you too will be judged. For in the same way you judge others, you will be judged, and with the measure you use, it will be measured to you. Why do you look at the speck of sawdust in your brother's eye and pay no attention to the plank in your own eye? How can you say to your brother, Let me take the speck out of your eye, when all the time there is a plank in your own eye? You hypocrite, first take the plank out of your own eye, and then you will see clearly to remove the speck from your brother's eye." (Matthew 7: 1-5)

Forgiveness takes work: the work of trusting your own value, of seeing the value of another, and of seeking reasons for the unacceptable behavior; the courage to ask for and receive forgiveness; and the willingness to renew the relationship and learn from your mistakes. It's difficult to admit when we are wrong, often because of the consequences for being wrong when we were children—not only the physical punishment but also the punishment of alienation and isolation caused by the people we were dependent upon. The Church has used that same punishment system and frightened people into ongoing dependence. It requires a confessional dependency that I hope you see is unnecessary.

NB: If you have the power and ability to injure, you also have the power and ability to set right the injury and reconcile the harm. Forgiveness doesn't require forgetting, but allows for the transformation of the hurtful act of another so you don't burden your life with the injury done to you. That's the power of your Christianity; but if you give that power away, your ongoing dependency on the Church is assured.

Hopefully, our discussion to this point has you seriously thinking about your independence from the Church and the responsibility you have for your spiritual life. I think the agrarian analogy of members being "sheep" and needing protection is inaccurate; it has lost its value for a twenty-first century Christian. The laity has allowed their lack of awareness and their dependency to lull them into a state of indifference about the power and responsibility they have over their spiritual lives. They need to wake up and accept the fact that they are responsible for their relationship with their Creator, and they must shift their thinking and act courageously to sustain the viability of their lives within a Christian Catholic community.

The next chapters will lay the planks for the bridge that may lead you back to a Christian Catholic community, beginning with the concept of authorship, which ends with your total acceptance and responsibility for your spiritual life. Before we move on, take a few minutes and reflect on the themes of this chapter.

Reflections

☑ You began life as an original blessing. Your value is not diminished but merely forgotten and distorted by unacceptable behavior that causes you and others injury and harm.

☑ You can't prove you are valuable. It's not an issue of proof, but of acceptance. Only problems with behavior can be solved. Your value is a condition of your existence.

☑ The extent of your ownership of the problem is the extent of your responsibility for finding and owning the solution.

☑ Forgiveness comes first from within and then is extended to another. Intermediaries in your confession can only consult, educate, or counsel. They can't forgive; they must not judge; and they should not determine punishment. Doing so removes the problem and its solution from you.

Expanding Your Knowledge

Read *Original Blessing*, in which Matthew Fox, a former Catholic priest and theologian, clearly identifies the difference between the two approaches to spirituality: fall/redemption vs. creation centered. Refer especially to appendix B in this book for an excellent summary. [7]

Read *Who Is Jesus?* by Richard Watts and John Dominic Crossan. [8]

Both J. D. Crossan's and Matthew Fox's books are intended to get you to think outside the nine dots of your Catholic education and not to be afraid to explore other resources that test your beliefs. The counterpunch to control, compliance, and indifference is courage, exploration, and education.

Puzzle solution:

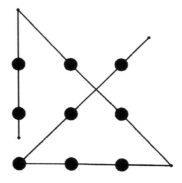

CHAPTER 3

AUTHORSHIP: THE JOURNEY TOWARD SELF-RELIANCE

My country did not send me 7,000 miles to start the race. They sent me 7,000 miles to finish it.
— JOHN STEPHEN AKHWARI

Long after the crowd had gone and the cameras had shut down, a lone runner entered the Olympic stadium to complete the marathon at the 1968 Mexico City Olympics. Injured earlier in the race due to a fall, John Stephen Akhwari of Tanzania stumbled along, and more than an hour after the others had finished, he crossed the finish line. When asked why he didn't quit when he was injured, he replied with the above quote—a quote that lives forever in Olympic lore. It encourages us to finish the race we have chosen, regardless of the pain, fear, or lack of reward that might accompany it.

No one told John Akhwari to get up and keep running after he fell. His desire and commitment to run and finish the race was fueled by a discipline and a state of consciousness forged in the long hours and commitment of long-distance training. This consciousness is what I call Personal Authorship. It involves a number of interrelated ideas that form a system of values and beliefs—as well as a focus for action—

when opportunities, problems, or challenges confront us. The concept is evolutionary and results in transitions that move us through the beginning dependency of childhood to an adult sense of maturity and responsibility for our lives. The key transitions are as follows:

- From acceptance and approval by others to self-acceptance and approval (self-worth).

- From learner to teacher/learner (self-improvement).

- From dependent to independent/interdependent (growth in interpersonal relationships as well as growth within a community).

- From passive acceptance of early beliefs to critical assessment of current beliefs (ownership for internal life).

- From blame and self-justification for actions to responsibility and accountability (ownership for public life).

- From being compliant to creating (personal goal determination).

Personal authorship is defined as: the recognition and acceptance of one's value, knowledge, skill, and commitment as it relates to any purpose, goal, or task. It's also the acceptance of accountability for any outcomes that result from the exercise of one's power and authority in pursuit of the purpose, goal, or task. As you peruse the definition, you see that it evolves from the concepts of:

- Original blessing, the recognition and acceptance of one's value;

- Problem ownership, the acceptance of accountability for any outcomes; and

- Forgiveness, (if required) as a result of the exercise of one's power and authority.

Let's break down and analyze the main components. To begin with, an *author* is one who creates, originates, or gives existence. Most notably, authorship is associated with those who create books, plays, art, and so on—and those of us who are creating our personal life story. By extension, *authorship* is the ownership and responsibility one has when creating or giving existence. To create requires power, and that power is used by the author, who exercises *authority*. Authority is the use of power to influence or command opinion, thoughts, or behavior. It derives from the Greek and means "from out of your own being."

Finally, to complete the foundation, we need to be aware of ideas surrounding the concept of personal power. Some of the best descriptions of how power is used can be found in Rollo May's *Power and Innocence*. Some of his descriptions help clarify how the Church wields power to control its members and foster their dependency. Personal power has two elements: the ability and choice to cause or prevent change, and the ability and choice to help or hinder the development of a relationship. There is no evaluation in this definition; the value assessment comes when the power is used and its effect on others is assessed.

Review the following uses of power as described by May, and examine the power options you use in conflicts, especially at home and work. Think about situations that you were responsible for and the consequences that arose from your actions. Then reflect on your experience of Church leadership and its use of power. Again, think about examples concerning you personally and consider what effect that use of power had on you.

Uses of Power

Exploitive: Subjects the weak to the strong with no concern for the needs of the weak. Tends to identify power with force.

Manipulative: Power over another that requires the collusion, collaboration, or cooperation of the weaker; probably out of some need in the weaker, of which the stronger may be aware.

Competitive: Power against another where the object is to win. The win/lose use of power tends to divide the community within which it takes place.

Nutrient: Power used for another to satisfy the needs of the other.

Integrative: Power used with another to build a better life for both. Uses the power of all to build community. [1]

No doubt, you can remember both positive and negative examples in the use of power in your interactions with others. The positive built a bridge to a relationship, enhanced self-worth, and created new opportunities for growth and well-being. The negative uses may have caused harm, ignored the value of the other, denigrated your sense of self-worth, or injured the reputation of another. The fact is, each of us has access to all the uses of power. Only awareness of the circumstances and conscious, informed choice not controlled by fear give us the potential to use our power in a way that is life affirming and healing for ourselves and others.

History is filled with positive and negative uses of power by the Church. However, *power exercised by the clergy is not our primary focus*. The important issue for us is *how we respond* to the power used by the hierarchy. If we collude with the use of hierarchical power, we allow our continued dependency on the Church and thwart our exercise of personal authorship. If we passively go along with the sanctions imposed or the accountability ignored when the Church uses exploitive or manipulative power, we collude and give tacit approval to continue the misuse. For example, when the Church controls people by using the fear of punishment in the afterlife, or protects clerics from the justice they deserve for abusing children, or refuses access to sacramental life for members using birth control or remarrying without Church permission, our failure to protest against these forms of control is colluding with the Church. The act of collusion is silent approval that continues the harm.

When we collude, we give up personal authorship, disengage from the issue, and give credence to the Church's stance by not stepping up and challenging it. Maybe we don't challenge it because we don't realize that we must hold ourselves accountable for our own spiritual life, for our ongoing learning, and for the choices we make as the author of our life. We've been taught that the clerical system and canon law decides these issues for us. But we are ultimately responsible for all aspects of our life. And to the extent we give that responsibility away, we denigrate our authorship and continue our dependency on the Church.

We are used to giving up responsibility to professionals, because we think they know better. Sometimes they do and sometimes they don't. We tend to give doctors control of our health, priests control of our spiritual life, and teachers control of our children's education. They do have authority that comes from their expertise—the authority of knowledge and skill. What they don't have with their parishioners, patients, and students is the authority that comes from another's authorship. The authority from personal authorship is based on the one who owns the problem and therefore must make the ultimate decision for his or her well-being by exercising that authority. The doctor can't force you to have surgery; the educator can't be totally responsible for your child's literacy; and the priest can't keep you from communion unless you agree to a control that he has no right to exercise.

Reflect back on the couple who used birth control and the argument created for their continued reception of communion. In that case, I acted as the one who had the authority of knowledge and skill, and I used the interpersonal skills of listening, feedback, and consultation to assist them with their problem. They, in turn, exercised the authority from their personal authorship, using their problem-solving and decision-making skills to make their decision. Why? Because they owned the problem and had to accept the consequences for their decision on a daily basis. I had no right to tell them what to do, to alienate them from sacramental life, or to scare them with unfounded, ambiguous punishment systems in the afterlife.

Self-Reliance and Personal Authorship

So, what's the work needed to commit to and develop a personal sense of authorship? Along with understanding and accepting the foundational principles of original blessing, problem ownership and forgiveness, there are three things necessary to achieve self-reliance and break your dependency on the Church.

1. An assessment of whether past beliefs (what you think or feel is true) are consistent with the elements

of authorship and whether they enhance your life now. Many beliefs we hold as adults were first formed and accepted in the intensity and/or frequency of childhood experiences that influence your behavior today. The question is, would you choose those beliefs today, especially if they could not stand the scrutiny of sound reasoning and emotional awareness that a mature adult would bring to the assessment?

2. A commitment to learn how and by whom those beliefs were generated and then to explore the beliefs that no longer affirm your value or the value of another. This requires you to look at your family of origin and the influence it still has on your behavior. If you were raised Catholic, explore your early Catholic training and its current influence on you.

3. A commitment to dispute the beliefs that injure yourself or another by keeping you imprisoned in a false certainty and thereby living your life under someone else's control and belief system. Most people act in concert with their conscious beliefs, but their unconscious beliefs also influence behavior. The question is whether those beliefs support your continued growth and provide a basis for personal authorship. If this sounds complicated, no worries, a clarifying example is coming up shortly.

Many books have been written on the formation of beliefs, so my intent is only to crack open a window on the topic and suggest that you not accept everything you think and feel as true, knowing you can change your belief when it doesn't serve your growth. The values and beliefs that sustain authorship—when others or institutions such as the Church act to keep us ignorant and dependent—are embodied in the following affirmations. Repeat these statements daily, and see if you find yourself reevaluating your relationship with the Church as well as your relationship with your health provider and any other social or educational authority.

- *Because I am an original blessing, I will intend no harm to myself or another.*

- *I have value, knowledge, and skill relevant to me, others, and the community.*

- *I am the first provider and decision maker when it comes to my physical, mental, and spiritual health.*

- *I am accountable for my continued learning.*

- *I choose the meaning and value of my life as it relates to all my experiences and circumstances.*

- *I accept responsibility and accountability for my choices. I do not blame.*

NB: For these affirmations to take hold, it's essential to understand how your beliefs were formed, the influence the unconscious has on your behavior, and the psychological and social environments that have influenced your personal development. It's not possible to cover this material here, but I've listed resource material at the end of the chapter that's eminently readable, informative, and interesting.

Undoing the Ties That Bind

Other than the power of love and forgiveness, I know of no more powerful force in the realm of human existence than the power of a person's belief system to enhance or disrupt the experience of one's life. William James, referred to as the father of American psychology, said, "The greatest revolution in our generation is the discovery that human beings, by changing the inner attitudes of their minds, can change the outer aspects of their lives." [2] In the horror and desperation of a concentration camp, Victor Frankl realized that the ultimate freedom was " to choose one's attitude in any given circumstance is to chose one's own way." [3]

It's important that we know whether beliefs we hold about ourselves in relation to the Catholic Church serve and support choices consistent with our authorship and choices that affirm us as Christian Catholics. Given this imperative, let's look at the framework and influence beliefs have on our lives.

Your beliefs are what you *think* and *feel* is true in the moment of an experience. They may not be objectively accurate regarding current reality, even though you may try to force them to fit an experience based on your need for protection, personal comfort, or certainty.

Conscious belief directs your actions. For example, as a fifteenth century sailor, I believe the world is flat and my boat will fall off the earth if I sail too close to the edge, so I sail only close to the shore. *Unconscious belief* also influences your actions. You're not aware of this belief, so when you behave ineffectively, you try to justify the behavior by making it consistent with the conscious belief. Say my son wants to be a sailor and explore the ocean, so he tells me he is joining an expedition headed up by a guy named Chris Columbus whose goal is to go "beyond the edge." I know the world is flat, and no one can change my certainty about this "fact," so I keep him from going to sea. The conscious argument is that the world is flat, so it isn't possible to sail beyond the horizon. And because I haven't done it, I know he can't do it.

However, the unconscious or unseen belief may be that I love him and I fear for his life. I may not realize this if all I want to do is control him and not own my problem: I fear for his life. So I use my parental authority to stop his dream, based on a presenting belief and rationale that prevents me from getting in touch with the true reason for my resistance. Therefore, the relationship between father and son is damaged; the father doesn't admit to his possible ignorance or fear, which creeps up and continues to create resistance when his son wants to break away, select life options that are risky, or move in any direction that frightens the father.

How Beliefs Develop

The process for understanding how we learn our beliefs is relatively simple. The complexity comes from the fact that who we experience ourselves to be has developed over a significant period. We know ourselves on several levels of awareness: physical, psychological, and spiritual. In addition, the early influence on our lives has a very strong effect on how we feel about ourselves today, even though most of it is on an unconscious or unseeing level.

As adults, we can deny that unmet needs of the past still influence us. It's difficult to recognize that we still seek the love and acceptance that we craved as a child. When this need wasn't recognized or nurtured properly by those responsible for our development, it left an emptiness that still lingers in us as adults. The Church has stepped in and tried to fill that void, but the love and acceptance is conditional on adhering, without question or dissent, to what its leaders say. It's a parental model stuck in immaturity that we adhere to as adults.

Here is an oversimplification of the process, but I think you will relate to the example. I've had many important people in my life. First, I had parents, grandparents, siblings, teachers, clergy, cops, and peers. As an adult, I have a spouse, bosses, physicians, priests, and peers. All of these people had and have an ongoing influence on me through the methods and intent of their communication.

It went something like this in early childhood: When I behaved in a way that was acceptable to an important person, I got a message: "What a good boy!" When I behaved in a way that was unacceptable, I got a message: "What a bad boy!" These people were making a judgment, albeit unintentional, about my self-worth—about whether I was lovable and acceptable—based on whether a *behavior* was acceptable or not. The problem is that children don't make the distinction between self-worth and behavior. Why? Because they aren't able to question the inappropriateness of the judgments that are being heaped on them.

Consider a child in a highchair who accidentally spills a glass of milk—or even wants to see what milk looks like as it falls to the floor. He is probably yelled at—"Why did you do that, bad boy. Can't you do anything right?"—at a decibel level that might shatter fine crystal. What goes on in the child's mind is not "Mom is having a bad day. She doesn't mean to say I'm bad or clumsy. She's upset with my behavior, and I'll forgive her and talk to her later about the attack I felt on my self-worth." No, the child hears and feels an unconscious generalization that he or she is dumb, stupid, and inadequate. If there is also a punishment system of alienation (I will not touch you physically or emotionally) or isolation (Go to your room; stay away from me) without reconciliation, a sense of separation can take place between the parent and child.

All these frequent or intense experiences are felt and remembered, albeit on an unconscious level, and saved in the conscious as well as the subconscious. Think of the iceberg that sank the *Titanic*. The ice under the surface did the damage. Now remember saying something you thought was harmless to a spouse or friend that was met with an explosive emotional reaction—so the punishment didn't seem to fit the crime. That's the *past* injury or insult hidden under the surface that springs out unexpectedly into the present. It is the cause of many an argument if it isn't recognized and managed effectively.

In addition, a judgment made by an important person, whether positive or negative, sends a message that my value is contingent on me behaving the way that person says is acceptable. What is more concerning is that I learn that my sense of value is dependent on someone external to me saying so. Even associating positive behavior with positive self-worth is flawed, because it may cause us to think, "If I can figure out what pleases the important people in my life, then I will be lovable." Anyone who has been married or worked for a boss who's a tyrant knows how impossible it is to meet another's unspoken or unclear expectations. So what we develop is a sense of self that learns to please others to confirm that we are lovable or competent.

The reverse may also happen: we test others, albeit unconsciously, by making mistakes or underperforming to see if we are still acceptable and lovable. Consider whether you fit any of the following descriptions or know of someone who does. (Most people can see that someone else is stuck but can't see themselves as stuck too.)

- People who fear failure and therefore never accept a challenge that could end in failure

- People who harm others because they hold different values and beliefs

- People who won't consider they may be wrong or may be seeing only a partial truth

- People who choose a life of dependency over self-reliance

- People who remain with a spouse despite physical and emotional abuse

- People who keep testing a loving relationship with unacceptable behavior to see if the other person will continue to love them

Depending on the frequency and intensity of the negative childhood experiences, we end up fearful, mistrustful of others, and predisposed to live out the beliefs and expectations of the important people who misguided us in our early learning. If this process goes unchecked and unquestioned, we protect what has been created and believed, whether positive or negative, effective or destructive. Why? Because it is what we have learned about ourselves, and it is all we have to explain who we are and how we understand and justify our presence in this life. It is called self-justification (you will find an excellent resource about this at the end of the chapter).

Finally, remember to be gentle and easy on yourself as you explore your past. You learned a lot that you couldn't defend against as a child but that you can take responsibility for today as past beliefs influence your current behavior. None of us had a perfect childhood, and therapists have made a great living helping people sort out what we learned in childhood. I suggest you read Ekhart Tolle's book *The Power of Now*, which will enhance your understanding of the process and the importance of dealing with and living in the present. Remember this bumper sticker: *That which you hold on to, holds on to you!*

The Church's umbilical cord

The Church has taken advantage of early learning that has enmeshed self-worth and behavior. It has done so by developing organizational beliefs to ensure control and compliance and to impede the consciousness of personal authorship. The foundational beliefs that support the Church institution and keep its members dependent include the following:

- The doctrine of the Magisterium, which controls all teaching and belief about Scripture, all of which is supposedly inspired

- The doctrines that define and control your sinfulness and process of salvation

- The scriptural interpretations and subsequent doctrines that provide the hierarchy with unilateral authority

- The doctrine of the infallibility of the pope

- Continued promulgation that the Catholic Church is the surest gateway to heaven (Actually, evolved human consciousness, not an institution, is the surest gateway to unity with God.)

Each of these doctrines is based on what the Church thinks about you and your spiritual state from birth. Its belief is that you were born a sinner; you need to be saved; you need its process of forgiveness for reconciliation; you must do what it tells you to do in all things it considers under its moral responsibility; and it will exclude you from the community if you don't toe the line concerning rules and regulations. If you do all this, then God loves you. Such a deal!

If you grew up believing this, it will take courage, awareness, and significant education to break from that structure. (It might also require extensive therapy and a robust Guinness now and then.) Yes, I'm suggesting that to be a good Catholic today, the price for the privilege is to give up your sense of personal authorship. If you give up personal authorship, you lose the life God created in you to understand, enhance, and live out fully.

The message of Jesus is clear: "I come that they might have life, and that they might have it more abundantly" (John 10:10). To allow an institution that perceives you as sinful and dependent on it for salvation and that assumes responsibility for your life is psychological and spiritual slavery you weren't created to endure. Finally, listen to the words of Jesus from the Scriptures: "Why do you not judge for yourselves what is right?" (Luke 12: 57).

Breaking the Gordian Knot

The Gordian knot is an exceedingly complicated problem or deadlock. It was an intricate knot tied by King Gordius of Phrygia and cut by Alexander the Great with his sword after hearing an oracle promise that whoever could undo it would be the next ruler of Asia. What I'm suggesting is a path to cut the Gordian knot created by the Church so you can be the ultimate ruler of your life. The sword we're going to use is doubt—doubt that leads to questioning, exploring, challenging, understanding, and ultimately disavowing others' judgments about your behavior and the effects of those judgments on your understanding of your value. In short, have the faith in yourself as a Christian to doubt the appropriateness of the judgmental role the Church has played and still insists on playing in your life.

We begin to reverse this old role of the Church by disowning—as someone else's mistake—the learning system you were raised with that says you are lovable and competent only when someone outside you says you are. The old beliefs are based on you trying to prove you're lovable and competent. It can't be done, so quit trying. For every expectation of others I try to meet, there are a million more that I don't know about. If you don't take anything else from these pages, take this:

NB: Your sense of self-worth is not something to be proven but to be accepted and experienced. You are valuable as a condition of your birth, as a part of creation that is here to learn and experience the mystery of life, and to assume responsibility for your efforts and results no matter how great or small the contribution in other's eyes. Take the path that you choose for yourself, not one imposed by the fear and ignorance of others. Most of all, know that your value is unconditional and that no one can take it away. Not even you can throw it away; you can only forget it for a while.

One process to understand and disavow the irrational beliefs that we learned is found in the rational-emotive system developed by Albert Ellis and Robert Harper in their book, *A Guide to Rational Living*. I'll list the reference at the end of the chapter if you want more explanation of the general process.

A Different Light on Scripture

After our discussion of beliefs, reflect again on Matthew 16: 18-20 and 28: 18, the two Scriptures that allow the

Church to give itself a unilateral power base. Do you still believe that a loving God created you with evolving consciousness and with the ability to be responsible for your own life, only for you to give that responsibility to a few men with unilateral power to control your life? Or, was that unilateral exercise of authority inserted into the Gospels and interpreted by a Church leadership to enhance their power and create a political system, whereby a mostly illiterate population could be kept under control?

Think about it, and while thinking, ask yourself if the parish priest or bishop is responsible for any aspect of your life? I hope your answer is a resounding no. If not, think about what issues you are willing to have them be responsible for and whether you freely gave them that responsibility? More than likely, a belief was created during your childhood and reinforced over time with ambiguous spiritual rewards and punishments that convinced you to give the Church responsibility for your moral actions and spiritual life. Remember, this same Church needed a doctrine of infallibility to protect itself from people asserting their right to think and act for themselves as they faced the ambiguous challenges of life. How do fallible men come up with the notion that the pope is infallible, if not to protect their dogma and control the beliefs of others? Fallibility is essential for growth. It creates a sense of humility—that we are open to learning. From the openness to say, "We might be wrong," comes a new awareness and acceptance of our life's challenges, and makes it possible to respond differently and with more flexibility.

Now, look at the Scriptures with a different focus. The Bible is not a single book but a library. It is an evolutionary study of God's covenant with creation. The understanding of God evolves as the history and wisdom of the people evolve.

If we do not accept our personal authorship, we are stuck with the interpretation and control of the Church. The New Testament Scriptures are filled with statements, parables, and instruction supporting our authorship. They speak of love and forgiveness, our oneness with God, the nonjudgment of ourselves and others, and our equality and unity with all other people. Other Scriptures and subsequent interpretations were probably inserted to build authority for the Church to control its members and survive in the social, economic, and political world of the time. If you accept the validity of your personal authorship, you may decide that past Church teachings that mitigate your responsibility for your life are not relevant benchmarks to decide how you live your life today.

If you're moving in the direction of accepting your personal authorship as the primary basis for choosing and accepting responsibility for all aspects of your life, what are the implications as you relate to the different aspects of the Church, such as clerical authority, dogma, and canon law? How much authority and responsibility for your spiritual life are you willing to accept as a creation of God? Are you willing to let a group of men, relying on historical teaching that they say is inspired, be the arbiter of your life? Will you act in concert with their proclamations just because they say they have the truth and the right to determine your moral decisions and actions? If you are still unconvinced, let me give some examples where Church teaching contradicts the love, acceptance, and forgiveness themes inherent in the Gospels and your personal authorship.

Spiritual Constructs

The Church says that baptism is essential if you want to go to heaven. It is so essential, there are different scenarios for adults who die before they are sprinkled with water but had the intent of wanting to be baptized. These people all get "saved". When it comes to a child, the Church isn't sure what happens and can only guess what process God might put the child through. (I'm not making this up.)

> As regards children who have died without Baptism, the Church can only entrust them to the mercy of God, as she does in her funeral rites for them. Indeed, the great mercy of God who desires that all men should be saved, and Jesus' tenderness toward children which caused him to say: "Let the children come to me, do not hinder them," allow us to hope that there is a way of salvation for children who have died without Baptism. [4]

The Church teaches this because of the previous statement about the need for children to be baptized:

> Born with a *fallen human nature and tainted by original sin*, children also have need of the new birth in Baptism to be freed from the power of darkness and brought into the realm of the freedom of the children of God, to which all men are called. [5]

There's the loop again. You start off sinful, even though you haven't done anything wrong and we, the hierarchy of the Church, are the only ones who can sell and insist on the spiritual insurance of baptism to make sure a child is saved. My question is, "From what?" You are now seeing the consequences of a doctrine based on original sin instead of original blessing.

Do you really want to entrust your spiritual assessment to and take guidance from any bishop or priest who can't proclaim that children who die without baptism definitely return to the loving God who created them? By the way, what distorted perception do they have of the loving God they are committed to serve who would make a child go through some sort of process before they enter heaven? If there was ever a time for spiritual certainty regarding original blessing, this is it. You can see the irrational belief system of the hierarchy in action when, during the pedophile scandal, bishops acted to protect the Church rather than act aggressively to protect the children.

Eucharist Inclusion

"And the scribes and Pharisees, when they saw that he was eating with sinners and tax collectors, said to his disciples, Why does he eat with tax collectors and sinners? And when Jesus heard it, he said to them, Those who are well have no need of a physician, but those who are sick. I came not to call the righteous, but sinners." (Mark 2:16-17)

"The Eucharist" has the most complex description of any sacrament. Although the Church states, as an article of faith, that Jesus is present in the Eucharist, it contradicts Jesus' intent as recorded in the Gospels. Mark shows that Jesus wants "sinners" to join him over a meal, which is exactly what faith in the Eucharist conveys. The Church took that simple invitation and surrounded it with a tollgate that has a big sign that reads, "The 'justified' Catholic only may enter." What the Church has done is "protect" the Eucharist from those they define as sinners, in clear violation of the gospel intent. Read what the Catholic Catechism says to justify exclusion:

Anyone who desires to receive Christ in Eucharistic communion must be in the state of grace. Anyone aware of having sinned mortally must not receive communion without having received absolution in the sacrament of penance. [6]

Why prohibit anyone, even those of other faiths who believe in the Eucharist as a source of spiritual strength, from joining in a Eucharistic celebration? The Eucharist is used by the Church as a "membership in good standing" gateway, when it should be a beacon for all to gather based on the invitation of Jesus: "Come to me, all you who are weary and find life burdensome, and I will refresh you" (Matthew 11:28).

There are many, many other examples in the Catechism whereby the gospel message of love and forgiveness is overridden by Church assertions and interpretations that insist on control and obedience to its dogma and teachings. The basis for this comes from the logic that says, "The word of God is inspired, and only we can determine what that inspired word means":

The task of interpreting the Word of God authentically has been entrusted solely to the Magisterium of the Church, that is, to the Pope and to the bishops in communion with him. [7]

The Church needs to control the Scriptures and their meaning to control its members. This control system has been responsible for actions that have justified killing and torturing people of other faiths, as well as those in their own community of believers, as in the insanity of the Inquisition. If you could ask Galileo what he thought about the Magisterium of the Church, you probably would have gotten a reply that couldn't be repeated in polite company.

Think about the Catholic parents of gay men and women. Their sons and daughters are living in loving relationships and may even be raising children, but the Church excludes them from the sacraments they were baptized in. I have never met Christian Catholic parents of gay children who have judged or alienated their children from their love as the Church has done.

Finally, if the Scriptures are inspired, why are there so many contradictions among the Gospel narratives? You would think clarity and unity of meaning would have been the criteria for the Holy Spirit's dictation system. Again, don't take my word for it. You can find plenty of examples if you review Bart Ehrman's works on interpreting Scripture, which I recommended earlier as important reading.

I suggest that inspiration is relational and that readers of the Gospels can glean the meaning of a passage based on personal study, openness, and willingness to listen to the community of believers. With in-depth Scripture scholarship and interpretation being accessible to anyone, through books, online sources, and other media, Christian Catholics have access to various resources to help them reach a meaning from spiritual texts that is relevant to their own lives. I suggest to you that the pope and bishops see revelation as finished, as stated in the Catechism, which is the first step toward the death of the message. Even more relevant is the notion that it is not in the Church's best interest for you to be educated and inspired and to take responsibility for your own spiritual life.

Your commitment to personal authorship may erode if you don't exercise responsibility for your own spiritual growth beyond the confines of the institution. Remember, you need to choose to be part of a community of believers instead of being obligated to be a part of an institution whose best days, given its inflexibility to reform, are probably behind it.

Courageous Authorship

My own introduction to what I now call personal authorship was incubated in the early days of my ministry as a hospital chaplain. I was visiting a woman dying of cancer, with
the thought that I might bring her some comfort. I quickly
realized she was well prepared for her next journey. I asked
her if she wanted the Sacrament of the Sick, a combination
of anointing, confession, and communion. She replied that
none of that was necessary, because she had reconciled herself
to the death that was coming.

Never giving up a chance to earn my salary, I said, "But
the sacrament may ease your suffering."

She looked me in the eye and said very gently but directly,
"Padre, I am in pain. I do not suffer. I am at peace with who
I am and where I'm going. Now, is there anything else I can
do for you?"

I at first felt hurt that I wasn't needed. My second reaction was a question: how did she figure this out? When I
asked her how she came to this place in her life, she said, "I
let go of everything and everyone that isn't relevant to the
journey I am about to take, except for the love I gave and
the love returned to me. Now, since your job is saving souls,
I can assure you that you're not needed, so, can you let go
of me?"

My feeble response was, "You got it."

Only later did I realize that she *did* have it. Because of her
willingness to strip everything from her past life that wasn't
relevant as she was dying, she was prepared for a journey only
she could take. By trusting herself and the lessons of her life,

she taught me that there is no one more powerful than those who can't be frightened—no one more powerful than those who accept total responsibility for their life.

William Blake strikes to the heart of the matter in transitioning from dependence on the Church to a life directed by personal authorship: "I must create my own system or be enslaved by another man's. My business is not to reason and compare, my business is to create." [8] This declaration requires us to affirm who we are in terms of our strengths, not our weakness. Motivation for change doesn't come solely by looking at those behaviors that are unacceptable and that we have judged as sinful. People change by drawing on their strengths and the belief in their value.

So, look at the behaviors called sinful and reframe them as mistakes of belief, separateness, and misinformation about yourself and another. That is the power of personal authorship. As a result, your sense of self can be described in the following reflections of beliefs about you and others. With these new beliefs, is it necessary to be dependent on the Church hierarchy, dogma, and the restrictions of canon law to determine the choices you will make for your moral and spiritual life? I think not. I hope not. I pray not.

Reflections on Beliefs about Myself and Others

☑ I am a loving, lovable, and competent human being.

☑ I am powerful and a choice maker.

☑ My choices involve creation and restructure, moving on and letting go.

☑ I am accountable for the outcomes and consequences of my actions.

☑ I can give and receive forgiveness, and I will remain open to doing so.

☑ I am accountable for my attitudes and responses—the good, the bad, and the ugly.

☑ I will seek to understand and accept the authorship of another.

☑ I act as the author of my life at all times.

There's a terrific quote often attributed to Nelson Mandela but actually written by Marianne Williamson in her book *Return to Love*. It encourages people to embrace their sense of authorship.

"Our deepest fear is not that we are inadequate. Our deepest fear is that we are powerful beyond measure. It is our light, not our darkness that most frightens us. We ask ourselves, who am I to be brilliant, gorgeous, talented, fabulous? Actually, who are you not to be? You are a child of God. Your playing small does not serve the world. There is nothing enlightened about shrinking so that other people won't feel insecure around you. We are all meant to shine, as children do. We were born to make manifest the glory of God that is within us. It's not just in some of us; it's in everyone. And as we let our own light shine, we unconsciously give other people permission to do the same. As we are liberated from our own fear, our presence automatically liberates others." [9]

If, at this stage of the discussion, you still don't believe that you can accept responsibility for what the Church has previously controlled in your life, keep working it, especially in the areas you are most resistant to accepting. The resistance is the edge of the known world you are sailing toward. Don't give up responsibility for your life. The only risk to you might be a slight tension headache and the loss of a night's sleep. Keep exploring, trusting, valuing, and learning about the most important person in your life.

However, if you find that you are willing to explore the exercise of personal authorship in your relationship with the Church, then you may want to consider how to work differently with other parishioners, clergy, and the bishop of your diocese to provide mutual support to one another. The concept of partnership—joining with others to revitalize your ownership of the parish community—is the logical extension of your personal authorship in developing interpersonal relationships for improving Christian Catholic action. Let's move on together!

NB: Before we go on, consider some advice. In his book, *Fire in the Belly,* Sam Keen recalls going through significant personal problems and seeking counsel from his friend Howard Thurman, whom he described as "a true witness, grandson of a slave, mystic, philosopher, a man acquainted with darkness and the journey of the spirit." Sam says Thurman's advice is the most important he ever received: "There are two questions a man must ask himself: The first is, 'Where am I going?' And the second is, 'Who will go with me?' If you ever get these questions in the wrong order, you are in trouble." [10]

As men and women searching for purpose, knowing and choosing where you are going is essential before you can invite others to join you or before you can join them. During our exploration of partnership, hold to your sense of authorship because, as we will see, it is the key to viable partnership.

Expanding Your Knowledge

I recommend *Mistakes Were Made but Not by Me: Why We Justify Foolish Beliefs, Bad Decisions and Hurtful Acts* by Carol Tavris and Elliot Aronson. [11] They focus on belief formation and why we find the need to justify ourselves, even when we're wrong.

A Guide to Rationale Living by Albert Ellis and Robert Harper gives an in-depth review of rational/irrational belief systems and the disputation of irrational beliefs. [12]

Also read Ekhart Tolle's *The Power of Now*. It guides you to experience exactly what the title suggests. [13]

CHAPTER 4

PARTNERSHIP: THE JOURNEY TOWARD INTERDEPENDENCE

If we are together nothing is impossible. If we are divided all will fail.
— WINSTON CHURCHILL

I was finishing my last year of theological studies at Catholic University in Washington, D.C. It was April 1968, and there were riots and fires throughout the city because of the assassination of Martin Luther King Jr. Our deaconate class was assigned to different parishes to practice our preaching skills and to give the parish priest a break. I was assigned to a mostly white church in Virginia, whose membership ran the gamut from "redneck conservative" to "bleeding-heart liberal," as characterized by the pastor. When I stepped up to the pulpit, you could cut the tension with a knife. It was the second Sunday after Dr. King's death, and the city was just getting back to some sort of normality; the fires were out, and the military had restored an uneasy order.

Partisan emotions among parishioners were running very high. I was supposed to preach on Matthew 18:20, which reads, "Where two or three are gathered in my name; there am I in their midst." I began by saying that there was possibly a mistranslation from the original Greek, so the text might have read, "Where two or three are gathered in my name, there is bound to be trouble." It was probably the need to break the tension we were all feeling rather than my own comic timing and delivery that caused the congregation to break into sustained laughter that wouldn't have been justified under any other circumstance.

Don't Try This Alone

That experience taught me that good people, including church people supposedly enriched by Scripture with the message of love and forgiveness, can be deeply divided on any issue affecting their values, faith, safety, or way of life. If you choose to return or remain in a Catholic community, be aware of the potential maelstrom you may generate as you bring your personal authorship to the task of changing the status quo of the parish. Remember, the Church is designed for self-protection, and it has many followers who have no interest in the changes we will be talking about as we lay out a path to reform.

The only work I should take on before attempting the change of an institution is the change of myself. Gandhi said, "We need to be the change we wish to see in the world," [1] which is my "self-work in progress." Once that progress has begun, change we want to create in the world is best generated by people of similar vision and dedication who are willing to form a system of mutual support. This system is called partnership, and it's a viable team model for like-minded Christian Catholics.

When you consider the rules and regulations, policies and procedures, power and influence the Church has over its community, it's a formidable undertaking to challenge its "ownership" of all things Catholic. If you try to use the command-

and-control, authoritative power model the Church uses, you'll end up creating an organization the Church knows how to defeat. Therefore, consider partnership; it's a management system the Church has little interest in using, but it could sustain an initiative for change if developed properly. The Church believes it supports partnerships, but its way of implementing this concept is really a smokescreen that hides the use of unilateral authority under the pretense of distributing responsibility, shared authority, and involvement in the work of the parish.

As you learn the definition of partnership, and the values and principles necessary to sustain it, you will see the discrepancy in the Church's idea of partnership. The sad thing is that even if there were a priest or bishop willing to enter into partnership with parishioners, canon law prohibits him from doing so, especially around the issues of authority and asset ownership. That's why a partnership system among the laity is essential if members are to confront the issues with the Church successfully and to direct change toward a collaborative organization.

As you read the key elements that define partnership, think about partnerships down through history and what they accomplished. Also think about your relationships and whether you've enjoyed a real partnership. People who come to mind in partnership endeavors are Bill and Melinda Gates, Hewlett and Packard, Lewis and Clark, Burns and Allen, Black and Decker, Ben and Jerry. I'm still struggling to identify successful partnerships in Church leadership. You will see why when we talk about how intention drives the relationships required for effective strategies, systems, and structures in an organization.

Basis for Partnership

A partner is one who chooses to share with another in the rights, responsibilities, and accountabilities necessary to achieve a goal. Partnership requires a relationship, mutually accepted by two or more people whose purpose is to commit their personal authorship in the achievement of an agreed-upon goal. The rights, responsibilities, and potential consequences are identified and, based on mutual agreement and commitment, are shared equally or equitably, depending on each person's contribution. Therefore, all parties must know

- one another's values, knowledge, skill, and commitment to personal excellence;

- that the goal includes a compelling purpose for all involved, and

- how work will get done and how people will work together in achieving the goal.

Unlike hierarchical models of organization, a partnership model has a clear system in which people enter and leave the partnership based on an invitation that is offered and accepted by individuals. These individuals also commit to use their personal authorship in achieving a compelling purpose and goal agreed to by the partners. In addition, partners have the right and responsibility to withdraw if they can't recommit when the purpose, goals, commitments, or values of the partnership change, or when their knowledge and skills are no longer relevant to goal achievement.

POP Diagnostic

Why are partnerships so difficult to implement? Because they are highly complex interpersonal relationships due to the makeup of the individuals involved. I created a model called the POP diagnostic to use with executives who were struggling with the balance between their work and personal life. I call it the POP diagnostic because it refers to the personal, organizational, and professional dimensions of our lives. Just look at what one person brings to the party.

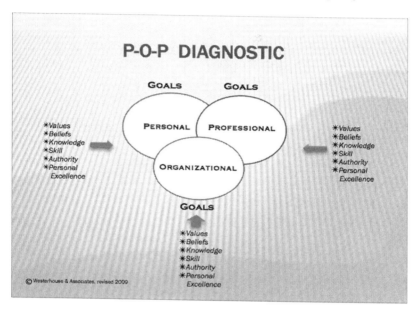

Definitions in the POP:

- Values: the guiding principles of life

- Beliefs: what we think or feel is true

- Knowledge: both formal and informal education

- Skill: the ability to apply knowledge

- Authority: the use of personal or positional power to influence or command opinions, thoughts, or behaviors

- Personal excellence: the application of self toward achievement of a goal that is challenging, freely chosen, and uses one's knowledge and skills to add value and achieve results within one's value and belief system

The *Personal* circle deals with the values, beliefs, knowledge, skill, and so on, that you hold in your personal life and that apply to the achievement of your personal goals. The *Professional* is the same in that it applies to your knowledge, skill, and so on, to the work you do in the world. The *Organizational* circle depicts your work and the position you hold while achieving an organization's goals. The circles are dynamic and overlap where the goals and priorities of one dimension of your life overlap and supersede the other two. The time and attention committed to goals among the three circles can be out of balance and in conflict because of the dynamics of change in all three areas.

No one has the POP in balance all the time; usually it's shifting dramatically due to high-stress events such as marriage, market changes, skill obsolescence, a death, the birth of a child, and so on. For example as a company executive, I may try to justify the harm I'm doing to my personal commitments by rationalizing my need to be consumed by work to provide a decent living for my family. Then again, I may simply have the need to massage my ego. Think about the shifts that have taken place in your life in each of the circles and what you did to bring your life back to some type of balance. Did you make the choices to reconcile the areas of conflict, or were the choices made for you?

A POP and a Parish

Try applying a POP to a parish situation. When we look at the knowledge and skill set of people in a Catholic community, we find a broad discrepancy between the priest and parishioners when it comes to management of the parish. The priest's charter is to preach the gospel and celebrate the Eucharist. In addition, the institutional Church has saddled the pastor with asset oversight and management of paid staff. How much time is he spending improving his professional education compared to the amount of time he spends managing the material assets, finances, and Church staff? Business people in his community who likely have more competence and effectiveness in those areas might be better managers and stewards of the assets while minimizing the organizational responsibilities of the priest.

Is true partnership between a priest and parishioners possible? Not likely, because *parishioners don't legally own any part of their community*. The bishop of the diocese controls revenues, assets, and even the power to select the priest. The parishioners own nothing. At best, parishioners have an affiliation with a parish, and even if they have a position in it, such as membership on the parish council, they have no ultimate authority to run the parish. The pastor must approve or can override every decision. If the pastor goes outside the policies of the diocese, he doesn't remain pastor for long.

Is partnership possible for parishioners? If they are going to take back their Church, *it's not only possible but necessary*. However, partnership is not an easy model to build or sustain due to the restrictions a priest or bishop can impose when his authority is threatened. When the laity challenges the clergy's authority over Church assets, they risk sanction, expulsion, and excommunication. A stunning example is the number of parishes that were closed due to the financial crisis precipitated by the abuse scandal. People lost long-term relationships with the parish and community in which they had been affiliated most of their lives. Because the community didn't own the assets, they couldn't stop the closure or impose any other solution. The excommunication of seven members of the board of St. Stanislaus Church in St Louis is a perfect example of abuse and intimidation by the bishop, which fortunately did not go unchallenged. The board refused to turn over the assets to the bishop and fought his control over governance of the parish. After seven years, the case is still being adjudicated.

NB: The Church's power to control its worldly assets is intoxicating and therefore is not something the clergy will let go of easily. Every Catholic should know that the abuse of organizational power by a bishop has no effect on one's spiritual life. Excommunication because of challenging the ineptitude, ignorance, or arrogance of the clergy over organizational or governance issues, must *not* affect your reception of the sacraments or your continued spiritual union with your community. Bishops and priests of integrity who are willing to challenge the misuse of power by their colleagues must teach this message. Bishops who use excommunication over issues of governance or asset control need to be confronted by people of principle who will use every legal means possible and every public media option at their fingertips. These bishops especially need to hear the loud and unmistakable noise that comes from Christian Catholics closing their checkbooks.

The Intentions of Partnership

If you enter a partnership to achieve a goal, statements of intention are necessary to seal the covenant among those who desire to work together for results. It's interesting to note that such intentions were the hallmark of the early Christian Church, albeit expressed differently. They are also the criteria that help individuals in the partnership assess their ongoing commitment and contribution to the goal. Here's an example:

- We mean one another no harm.

- We accept and understand one another's values, beliefs, knowledge, skills, and commitment, relevant to the partnership and its purpose and goals.

- We support one another's physical, mental, and spiritual health.

- We support one another's ongoing learning.

- We determine authority of position based on the authority of knowledge and skill applied to the current issue.

- We commit to a process of mutual support during the life of the partnership.

My first experience with being confronted by the intentions of partnership came as I started a new job as vice president of human resources at a medical technology firm in Palo Alto, California. I was introduced to the executive assistant, who also supported the CFO of the company. I invited her to discuss how she wanted to work together, and she said that having a partnership where we helped one another get work done was her preferred style. I said great, and after a few more points of clarification about my schedule and workload, we went to work.

About three hours into the day, I needed a break and some coffee. An hour earlier, I had given her a draft of a presentation to prepare for an afternoon executive team meeting.

I walked out of the office, saw that she was working on my project, and said, "I would like some coffee, please."

She quickly replied, "So would I. Black with two sugars, please," and continued to type.

To say the least, I was surprised but had the good sense to say "Okay." I didn't think that would be her response, but it was the absolute right response because she was working to get me prepared on time and also needed a coffee break. It made no sense to stop her so my ego or positional status could be served.

Having the authority of position requires you to serve those who have the authority of knowledge and skill. Otherwise, you impede work being done and goals being achieved. The CFO and I walked together to the afternoon executive meeting. I know he heard the exchange around the request for coffee, because he said, "I see you've met who we actually work for."

Why Partnership Is the Basis for a Christian Catholic Community

I selected partnership as my management model of choice to show that it is the more effective model in dealing with the complexity of the transition we will talk about in the chapter on the path to reform. I'll give you a sneak peak at where the governance issues of the current diocese and parish model need to shift to build a Christian Catholic community.

Using the partnership criteria as a foundation, like-minded parishioners would gather in partnership and commit to create the intentions and goals for building a Christian Catholic community. The intentions and goals become the focus for developing the strategic initiatives to begin the transition from the current state of the governance of the parish to a future state of shared governance. Here are some intentions and goals of a partnership that would cause acid reflux in the bishop and priests of a diocese:

- From a hierarchical model of control to a stewardship model of service. The community calls the priest to educate and to celebrate with it for a period and then he moves on.

- From church ownership of assets to lay ownership of assets. The community owns and is responsible for management of its church's assets.

- From centralized clerical control of the Catholic community to lay governance within the Christian Catholic community. The most competent in the community manage assets.

- From autocratic diocesan governance of parishes to parish council governance with asset distribution and the mission of the community determined by clergy and parishioners. That ministry (meeting the identified needs of the members of the community) is the responsibility of all. Any role within the community is open to all without bias as to gender, age, or sexual orientation, assuming the person has the necessary education and experience.

If you accept these intentions and goals, or some variation, as examples of what might be necessary to move to a Christian Catholic community, it follows that partnership is the best way to fulfill the goals emanating from the intention. Why? Because partnership, by definition, provides the equality of interpersonal relationships, systemic parameters regarding use of power and authority, and, most importantly, a commitment to ownership of the goals and resources of the Catholic community. Any other structure—such as the unilateral, autocratic system the Church is using—doesn't allow for shared responsibility and authority. Therefore, you don't own it, you won't be allowed to take responsibility for it, and you end up being in a community without participation in the crucial areas of financial management, asset distribution, goal setting, and selection of people to engage in ministry.

By my definition and the restrictions of canon law, priests are not allowed to enter into partnerships with the laity, so the *laity must decide if they want partnership to be the structural relationship they will use to take back ownership of their parish.* However, parishioners must go in with their eyes wide open about the roller-coaster ride that comes with the stages of developing a highly effective partnership. Some say managing partnerships is a little like making sausage, which is not something we will describe in case you're eating while reading. There are five nonlinear, emotionally charged stages in building effective partnerships. (You can find an outline of this process in appendix A for future reflection and for an understanding of the energy and resources needed to sustain a partnership.)

Managing Partnerships

Although the development of a partnership can be challenging, do all partnerships need to go through the angst of the stages described in appendix A? The answer is no, if there is a series of process checks and interventions at critical "pinch points." A pinch point is a transition event that can cause disruption and significant conflict if the values, management systems, and communication process for the partnership aren't in place to minimize the pain that's felt. The key transition events of partnerships include the following:

- the formation of the partnership;

- a new partner entering or a current partner leaving;

- a change or challenge to any of the "intentions" criteria;

- a change in the charter or goals of the partnership;

- a failure of the partnership structure and the use of power to meet the challenges.

Partners can do several things to minimize the disruptions such transitions can cause as a group works toward a goal. These interventions require that the partners be conscious of their thoughts, feelings, and actions as they engage in the work of the partnership. Each partner must be willing to accept feedback from other partners on her or his behavior in a forum that provides periodic, face-to-face meetings to address pinch points. This process should be a piece of cake for those living the gospel message and the intentions of authorship and partnership.

- Periodically conduct a POP diagnostic goal audit among the partners to ensure that conflicts in the personal, professional, or organizational arena are revealed and resolved.

- Review the goals established by the partnership. Advise one another of the progress and problems toward goal achievement.

- Make sure leadership of position rotates based on knowledge and skill as well as technical or managerial ownership of the problem.

- Give specific feedback to one another on individual performance towards goals. Since relationships are built on positive feedback, make sure there is more positive than corrective feedback during these meetings.

- Adjust strategies, tactics, plans, or resources to resolve problems. Assimilate new solutions or adjusted milestones.

There is a lot to pay attention to in maintaining a partnership, and the success of it is contingent on the partners paying attention. A check-and-balance system based on periodic effective feedback and mutual support can help partners pay attention. A partnership's sustainability doesn't depend on one person. It can deflect a threat or challenge only if the partners support each other and partners' skills are used effectively.

Letting Go

Before we move on to collaborative organizations, which will align the concepts of authorship and partnership, let's explore the process of change. Earlier I mentioned that "life is change, but growth is optional". That quote reminds me to choose authorship, no matter what happens in my life. We know change is inevitable and necessary for life to evolve. What we do with the experience of change is our choice and responsibility, and it will determine whether we grow to new awareness or get stuck in the same old drama.

To be unstuck, we must first grieve. We need to let go of past beliefs, past experiences, past fears, and the past certainties that impede our growth. It's said that people don't fear change; they fear the loss that comes with change. Areas of loss include the following:

- Security—loss of control, knowing the future, or where you fit in the scheme of things

- Competence—not knowing what to do, whether your knowledge and skills will be viable in the new context, be it family, work, or church community

- Relationships—the familiar relationships, clear roles, and the sense of belonging you relied on in the past especially in your parish

- Direction—a sense of where you're going and why, including a sense of meaning and purpose that was determined by others in the past

- Territory—the loss of a physical space and location that's familiar, such as a Catholic parish or school

Now add the loss of belief, certainty, and trust in the Church that you thought was ensured. These losses are valuable because they open up plenty of room to access the courage to build a new relationship with your Christian Catholic community. According to both change theory and the stages of grieving, you first experience states of denial and resistance, which keep you stuck in the past. Then come states of exploration and refocused commitment that propel you to the future. Take the first step and grieve the loss of the beliefs, relationships, and comforts that keep you stuck in someone else's control.

NB: If you are male and were told at a young age that "big boys don't cry," grieving can be difficult for you to access. Crying is an indication of hurt, loss, anger, or fear. If you suppress the trigger mechanism of grieving, namely crying, you block access over time to the feelings surrounding grief.

When that grief is bottled up, it can create all sorts of havoc on your physical, emotional, and spiritual health, to say nothing of your close relationships. Don't fear grief; it's the light that exposes the loss.

Two excellent resources, one by William Bridges and the other by Cynthia Scott and Dennis Jaffe, mentioned at the end of this chapter can give you a deeper understanding of the dynamics and process of personal change. Please consider reading them if our discussion thus far has you uncertain about your direction. Regardless of whether you commit to work on changing your parish community or diocesan organization, this information will be a great help in any change process you come across in your life. Now take a moment and reflect on the focus of this chapter.

Reflections

☑ We have chosen this partnership freely and will work together in a spirit of mutual support.

☑ We will understand and commit to a goal and to each person's contributions toward its achievement.

☑ We will not intentionally harm one another or the environment in the achievement of the goal.

☑ We will assess the viability of the partnership if
∞ the goal changes or is no longer compelling;
∞ the knowledge or skill set required changes; or
∞ the will to continue changes.

☑ We will agree to accept the rewards or consequences of our actions as equal or equitable partners, depending on prior agreement.

☑ We will affirm and honor individual authorship, even at the loss of the partnership.

This chapter is a tipping point. If you can believe in and accept the total responsibility that comes with your authorship, you can leave the hierarchal model of Church and continue to search for a truly Christian community. In addition, if you choose to participate in the Church's reform, you can work to develop partnerships within your parish. Either way, you have taken a step closer to the freedom the gospel message proclaims. Now you have a clear choice to move on, outside the confines of the Catholic Church, or move back in to the parish community to start the real work of reformation.

However, be aware that when we offer the strategic initiatives for change in the final section, the clash of ideas and strategies will cause a "white cell response" from the Church's clerical system, which will see you as an intruding virus that needs to be controlled from spreading to the rest of the "body."

As we continue on to the discussion of collaborative organizations, you will face countless opportunities and choices; you will need to determine whether holding on to past beliefs, relationships, fears, or dependencies is relevant to the journey ahead. Affirming your authorship by grieving, letting go, and dying to the obstructive beliefs of the past is essential in developing partnerships so you can join with other parishioners in moving toward your Christian Catholic community.

Expanding Your Knowledge

The following books are good and necessary reads if you feel any "dis-ease" as we move forward to the section on collaborative organizations.

Peter Block, *Stewardship: Choosing Service over Self Interest* (San Francisco Berrett Kohler 1993). This book will give you a clear read on the value of partnership as a way to enhance service leadership, and to use partnerships as a basis to deliver product and services. If you decide to engage in the work of reform, this work will definitely help you prepare for the challenges. [2]

William Bridges, *Transitions: Making Sense of Life's Changes*, (Perseus Publishing, 1980) [3]

Cynthia Scott and Dennis Jaffe, *Getting Your Organization to Change*, (Menlo Park, Crisp Publications, 1999). [4]

The works of Bridges and Scott/Jaffe are excellent on dealing with change and are a good read. They have captured the basic elements of personal and organizational change that has survived the test of time.

CHAPTER 5

COLLABORATIVE ORGANIZATIONS: THE JOURNEY TOWARD A CHRISTIAN CATHOLIC COMMUNITY

Sometimes I lie awake at night and ask, "Where have I gone wrong?" Then a voice says to me, "This is going to take more than one night!"
— Charlie Brown
Charles M. Schultz, *Peanut's Quotes*

After a difficult meeting on Capitol Hill, President Dwight Eisenhower entered his vehicle and his driver asked him where he wanted to go. The president was reported to have said, "Anywhere, son, there's trouble all over this town."

The Church has significant trouble with its policy, practices, and personnel on a wide swath of its organizational landscape. There's no end to the issues we could address, but there is no hope of reform if the pinch points aren't addressed in a way that either transforms those in leadership or shows that if they want to survive, it's in their best interest to get on board a train that's leaving the station. Where do you start transforming an organization that resists change and, when forced to move, slides at less than glacier speed? Let's look at another slice of the POP diagnostic for insight.

Personal	Professional	Organizational

EXCELLENCE	PROFESSIONAL vs BUREAUCRATIC		IMPERATIVES	
* Clear understanding of the goal	*Areas of knowledge & skill	* Rules & regulations, policies & procedures	*Vision	* Tomorrow
* Personal choice of the goal	* Solve problems, make decisions based on knowledge & skill	* Solves problems, makes decisions based on rules & regulations	* Mission	* Today
* Application of knowledge & skill			* Core Values	* Principles of the promise
* Achievement of results	* Authority comes from knowledge & skill	* Authority comes from position	* Willingness to change	* Potential for growth
* Mutual support				

© Westerhouse & Associates, revised 2009

In this chart, we see the conditions necessary for people and organizational systems to be effective. It explains the reasons why the Church is in such trouble, especially concerning its priests and professional lay staff. This chart illustrates the criteria for personal excellence, the basis for tension in a professional working in a bureaucratic organization, and the essential components for organizational viability in a competitive marketplace. Let's explore each one:

Personal excellence. The literature illustrates four elements people must have to experience a sense of accomplishment and a fifth element that's necessary to evoke excellence in teams. This process is straightforward. People in partnership must understand the goal; choose the goal; have knowledge and skills to add value to goal achievement; and see results because they added their value. The fifth element is giving and receiving mutual support as a result of teamwork. This process holds for both clergy and laity.

Organization imperatives. I'm jumping to the other side of the chart because the middle holds the greatest conflicts and needs more clarification. The four essentials for *organizational viability* are the following:

- Vision: We speculate on what lies ahead for tomorrow, and we plan for it.

- Mission: We know what is required for today, and we do it.

- Core values: We, as leaders, know the promises we need to keep to our parishioners, employees, and stakeholders to keep their trust in our product or service.

- Willingness to change drives the potential for growth: Other churches will attract Catholics to their communities because of their ability to adapt to the psychological and spiritual needs of people as they wrestle with the challenges of today's world. Rigid dogma is the first sign of death for an organization that can't or won't adapt to the needs of an intelligent person adhering to their sense of authorship.

Think about whether the Church has a clearly articulated vision and mission statement that it promulgates in understandable language that all can embrace. Does it adhere to the core values (the abuse scandal gives it a big black eye on that one) and hold people accountable for ignoring those values? Finally, is the Church open to change to enhance its outreach to the disenfranchised, who have every right, according to the gospel, to participate fully in a Christian Catholic community?

Professional vs. bureaucratic. Most conflict arises in the interface between the professional response to work and the bureaucratic controls. Why? We expect professionals to solve problems and make decisions based on their knowledge and skill. Their authority comes from that expertise. Their primary responsibility is to be effective when delivering services. The concept of bureaucracy, which goes back to early Roman times and was articulated by Max Weber, a German sociologist of the early twentieth century, has a contrary purpose. Weber pointed out that a bureaucratic system of organization is based on rules and regulations; policies and procedures are used to solve problems and make decisions; and the one who has the position of running the bureaucracy holds authority. The focus is primarily on efficiently meeting the goals and the mission of the organization with the least possible expenditure of resources. People don't necessarily have to be competent to run a bureaucratic organization, as evidenced by many appointed government bureaucrats and by diocesan bishops in legal and financial trouble.

There are enough gaps and tensions in this chart to place the Church's organizational viability and effectiveness at significant risk. Let's look at some of the pinch points, beginning with the professional/bureaucratic.

Whom Do I Serve?

When priests and bishops look at the chart, they have to ask themselves, "Was I ordained to preach the gospel or to sustain the Church organization?" They may say, "Both," but what happens when their personal commitment to the gospel is thwarted by the bureaucracy? The abuse scandal is a perfect example of bishops covering for priests and ignoring justice for the injured to protect the reputation of the Church. Priests who counsel people to adhere to Church teachings even when it's injurious to people's lives are serving the bureaucracy, not the gospel.

As a professional, the priest is to coach, educate, and facilitate a person's choice toward owning and accepting responsibility for an issue without passing judgment or causing alienation or isolation. The bureaucratic model has all the predetermined solutions for major issues surrounding life and death as well as inclusion in or exclusion from the Christian community. This leaves little room for professional competence to play a role in alleviating suffering. What you end up with are priests who fail to help people make critical judgments, and they give up their own professional responsibility in favor of a set of rules and regulations cemented in canon law. Talk about being trapped between the organization you represent and a gospel and people you are ordained to serve!

How does a priest have a sense of personal excellence when his judgments or social status is controlled by the bureaucratic model? A good priest today has to push back constantly on the ever-encroaching policies and practices of ministry coming out of Rome that demand a more conservative approach and insist on doctrinal purity. If he is gay, he is estimated to be one of between 25 to 45 percent of priests discriminated against by his own Church. So, where does a gay priest find mutual support and understanding in a celibate priesthood when his sexual orientation is not only a basis for alienation but also deemed sinful, if practiced, by his own Church leaders, some of whom are also gay. When I asked a gay priest why they don't rise up and become a power base in the Church, his only response was that he, and others like him, are afraid of being thrown out of the only work they know how to do and the only work they are committed to doing. There's that punishment system again, with its threat of economic, psychological, and spiritual alienation and isolation.

Finally, today's priest has to try to connect with a future vision of a church whose membership is decreasing in many geographical segments, whose priests are aging and retiring, and whose leadership is largely unwilling to change. In addition, in the media he sees colleagues and leaders undermining the core values of the gospel instead of being good stewards in proclaiming and acting in concert with those values. It's not an exciting future that entices bright, creative people to consider and embrace a call to ministry.

Working in Tandem

There is a tension between the professional commitment of a priest to the gospel and the people he serves, and the bureaucratic policy of the Church that is enforced by those holding positional power. This tension is a necessary component to deliver services and products effectively and efficiently in large multinational organizations. This is not in dispute. What is in question is how to balance the value and effectiveness of the professional with the efficiency and timeliness that the bureaucracy provides. The key is to make sure the bureaucratic organization is adaptive and oriented to serve the professional who is providing a service. Let's look at the model of a collaborative organization as a possible solution to ensure appropriate flexibility of the bureaucracy so that it is aligned with the service needs of parishioners. This model includes the following elements and definitions:

Collaboration, working together, can be broken down into two types:

- Functional collaboration: the contribution of knowledge and skill toward goal achievement

- Personal collaboration: the commitment of personal authorship to support others in partnership to achieve a purpose or goal

Organization is an integrated set of subsystems involving the use of human and material resources to achieve a goal. The subsystems are typically structural, technical, social, and managerial.

If we combine these elements, we come up with the following definition: a *collaborative organization* is a group of people committed to a purpose or the achievement of a goal by using the author/partner values and principles, and who choose implementation strategies, systems, and structures that are internally noncompetitive.

Although you are aware of the author/partner principles that insist on ownership of problems and on mutual support for group members, it's important to note the last part of the definition: strategies, systems, and structures that are internally noncompetitive. The importance of this last phrase can't be underestimated, because in our culture we have been raised to compete. Competition undermines the author/partner principles necessary to confront the Church's leadership. Let's look at the definitions and consequences of competition, and it will become clear why a competitive environment doesn't fit a collaborative organization.

Competition

Competition is a contest between rivals. A contest is a struggle for superiority. Rivals are two or more people or entities striving to reach or obtain something that only one can possess.

Given these descriptions, if you have a church culture made up of strategies, structures, and systems that are competitive in design and enforced by unilateral power, you have built in a potential for conflict over goals and resources. If the priest wants to build a new church, but the people want to use their resources to develop outreach to the poor, who wins? The person with the power makes the rules. You can't compete head-to-head with the current hierarchical structure; you will lose. What you can do is work around the structure, and we will discuss how to achieve that in the levers and interventions for reform.

Consider the possible implications of competing against a clerical system that has no qualms about using manipulative and exploitive forms of power. In a recent case in Arizona, Bishop Thomas Olmsted, who oversees the Phoenix diocese, withdrew from St. Joseph's Hospital both its designation as Catholic and its affiliation with Catholic Health Care West. He did so because of the hospital's decision to terminate a pregnancy that posed serious health risks to the mother. He also prohibited the Mass, and removed the Eucharist from the hospital's chapel. Here is a man with no authority of knowledge and skill abusing his authority of position and superseding the judgment of physicians who chose to save the life of the mother. This is an example of the unbridled arrogance of positional authority that, if unchecked and unchallenged, causes harm on many levels, including the psychological abuse for all accused. This "minister of the gospel" betrayed the message of love and compassion in the gospel. Why didn't he seek to understand the difficult decision the physician and his colleagues made, and quietly console and teach them in private? Instead, he used the public media to punish all involved, and conveyed to the world his so-called righteous use of positional power. What he also conveyed in this instance was his abject failure as a priest.

This bishop missed the mark and clearly did not act according to the words of Jesus to forgive. Who will hold him to account? Why won't the Christian Catholics of Phoenix ask for his removal and close their checkbooks until he is removed? There is nothing sadder or more dangerous in the institutional Church than ignorant and arrogant people holding positional power. As history attests, the damage to the People of God can be significant.

Service vs. Competition

Service to others is not a competitive model of organization unless you set up systems for reward and punishment among those who are serving. The goal of good service is to make sure the customers get what they need, when they need it. If bishops and priests took an attitude of service to rather than control over its members, there would be no basis for competition with their members. However, when bishops think they are in a contest for survival or that they need to seek an advantage over an opponent, they play to win. They are competing for approval from the pope or his minions in Rome, for popularity with the people who support their diocese financially and politically, or for the next biggest diocese or the red hat of a cardinal.

Here's what competition can generate within a Catholic community:

- The unilateral misuse of positional authority to override the authority of knowledge and skill. The one with the power always wins. If you don't agree, you lose.

- Systems of priority setting, problem solving, and decision making based on power politics and leadership control rather than on requirements for resourcing goal achievement based on the vision, mission, and core values.

- Major tension between the bureaucratic model of organization and the professional standards of service, with significant leaning toward the bureaucratic way of handling conflict and solving problems.

Now consider the effect this environment has on the people working in a Church organization. People who work in a win/lose organization have a tendency to be insecure at work and mistrusting, because pleasing the one in power or winning his or her approval is the basis for acceptance. As we discussed before, pleasing others is a constantly changing target and sets you up for failure. You learn not to express feelings, needs, or wants for fear of punishment by isolation or alienation. Finally, you allow others to set goals for your life and determine what success means. Is this part of your parish life? Do you give deference to a priest or bishop even when they are wrong? Do you challenge the unacceptable behavior of a priest or bishop and hold them to account?

If you have among clergy and laity unacceptable competitive behaviors that undermine the service to the parish, know that it will also erode the collaborative systems intended to sustain and enhance the service. What is clearly needed is a shift from competition to collaboration, beginning with those committed to service leadership as the model for partnerships. That shift requires a good understanding of what the principals of authorship and partnership are and how they help build and sustain an environment of mutual support, safety, exploration, and achievement.

If we don't compete, what are the systems and structures that support partnership as a basis for collaborative organizations? They're called high-performance teams.

Team Effectiveness: A Moving Target

Many a tree has fallen and many a gigabyte has been used to discuss teamwork. A blind man throwing a dart at the business section of a bookstore would likely hit a book on building teams. I'm only going to hit the highlights, but I'll offer references at the end of the chapter for your continued study. Let's review what the literature suggests are the characteristics of these teams and how they complement effective partnerships. As you read the didactic part of this information on teams, let your mind float to an assessment of whether low-performance or high-performance teams are common in your diocese or parish.

NB: All teams are dynamic and never static. They are subject to the second law of thermodynamics; they lose energy to a maddening degree. Once you think you have it right, it shifts, and team members find themselves competing with one another. Although they say there is no "I" in team, there is an "A," and that stands for authorship. Don't ever give up your sense of authorship to stay with a team. It's too costly to your spirit and won't fulfill the purpose of your life.

Low-Performance Teams

Most of my work with corporations was because of an inability of their teams to function well. In the nineties in

Silicon Valley, hundreds of high-tech start-ups were created by capital investment firms and nurtured by incubators to get them started. On average, seven out of ten of these companies failed. Of the ten companies I worked with; only two made it to a viable place in the market and are still thriving today. Although that record may say something about my consulting skills, I usually walked in to a company with a stake already planted in its economic heart. Regardless of whether they had a potentially viable product, when I arrived on scene, I found that the threads of their destruction were already sewn into the fabric of their organization. I found several characteristics of low performance permeating their teams. (See appendix B for a comprehensive list. Use it to assess the current state of your parish or diocese.)

High-Performance Teams (HPT)

High-performance teams exhibit the opposite characteristics of low-performance teams, and are usually found in highly functioning operations such as specialized military units and "first to market" product development organizations. However, they take a ton of work and mental and emotional maturity to keep from eroding into disorder that impedes success. (See the characteristics of HPT listed in appendix C.)

Teams with these characteristics have a high value for serving their customers with a high-quality product or service. Although the notion of "customer" may not seem relevant to a parish, the values and systems that organizations put in place to serve customers, especially after the sale of a product or service, provide a helpful model for a parish or diocese. Parishioners who need access to a food pantry, sacramental rituals, home visits, and so on, can be better served if those offering the service understand the requirements of an effective service model.

In addition, HPTs require accountability from every member of the team. For example, how often do you hear a priest present the message of the gospel with conviction in a way that educates you, enlivens your spirit, and helps you deal with the challenges of your daily existence? If people gave according to the quality of sermons, the church's monthly revenue stream would flow to a trickle in many parishes. If there were systems in place for parishioners to give feedback to the priest on his sermons, he might be encouraged to reflect and prepare more thoroughly, especially if the pulpit was ready to be assumed by others in the community who were willing and able to preach the gospel more effectively. Ongoing assessment and corrective action of every member of an HPT is critical to meet the service expectations of the community, and that means corrective feedback to the priests and bishop.

Stop the Drain of Talent and Treasure

I have friends and relatives raised Catholic who have shifted to churches with multimedia, psycho/spiritual, entertainment services. When I asked them if they had any idea how many of the members were ex-Catholics, their nonscientific guess was that between 20 to 30 percent were disenfranchised Catholics. These are huge churches with three to four thousand people in attendance every Sunday. In addition, more Hispanics, which accounted for much of the recent growth of Catholicism in the United States, are leaving for Protestant, evangelical churches. Any business losing that much of its customer base would take a critical look at its key organizational elements—staff, strategy, systems, and structure, as well as product and services. An enterprise with these losses would be out of business quickly unless it had an addictive product distributed by a cartel.

I can only assume the Church isn't interested in an organizational assessment because it wants only a certain type of Catholic: one who is dependent, loyal without question, and remains quiet even with the incompetent administration of resources. All the while, the bishops want to see donations increase every Sunday to mitigate bad decision making and choices that have brought on significant debt. That may sound harsh, and it's intended to, because the Church doesn't meet the conditions for viability we spoke of earlier, yet parishioners continue to put good wine into old wine skins. They keep paying for what they will never own, so I can only surmise they are too frightened or too caught up in old beliefs and habits to risk separation from the organization.

People of God—Throw Open the Windows

I believe the People of God and the Spirit that resides within the Church can't possibly condone the current state of the institution. Furthermore, I believe the Spirit is directing a wellspring of ideas and challenges through the increased consciousness of a laity that can't be ignored any longer. I recommend a book by Margaret Heffernan, *Willful Blindness: Why We Ignore the Obvious at Our Peril,* that explains the blinders Church leaders have concerning the current problems of the Church. The premise of the book suggests that we tend to deny the truths that are too painful, too frightening, or too threatening to admit. The Church's leadership has obstructed the revelation of the uncomfortable truth that priests abused children and bishops covered it up. It also continues to disenfranchise gay priests, to exclude women from full participation in sacramental life, and to maintain that marriage is antithetical to a priestly vocation. My conclusion from the author's treatise is that, if Catholics of conscience want to see change in their communities, they need to wake up, take off the blinders, and get in the game. Christian Catholics need to collaborate to identify, own, and meet the needs of their communities. Peaceful but active resistance is necessary for the laity to regain responsibility for their spiritual lives and control over the assets of their parishes. This kind of resistance has all the hallmarks of the civil rights movement of the sixties and will be equally as challenging.

So, if your anxiety level hasn't gone up a notch, you may not have understood what I'm suggesting as a path to reform. Be assured that all competencies necessary to begin this reform already exist in most Christian Catholic communities. The laity must be courageous and hold firm to what they want if they seek intentional reform. And if they don't...

Reflections

The building blocks for accepting personal responsibility for your spirituality are in place. And the ingredients for initiating organizational reform—authorship, partnership, and collaborative teams—have been presented and discussed. These concepts offer you the choice to help the Church make some shift toward the following:

☑ Create noncompetitive high-performance teams to sustain a collaborative community.

☑ Distribute the work of the parish to the most competent, and invite all to share in the vocation of ministering to others.

☑ Own what you have paid for and build a legacy of stewardship to others in need, sustained within the Christian Catholic community.

Before continuing to the path for reform, ask these two questions: (1) Do I feel any ownership for the Catholic Church community I participate in? and (2) Do I want to align with others in partnership to move the parish or diocese toward a more Christian Catholic community?" Before you turn the page, sit with the experience of who you are in relation to the Church and its leadership. Consider an admonition Peter Block makes in his book on stewardship: "If there is no transformation inside each of us, all the structural change in the world will have no impact on our institutions." [1]

Go back and reread the "Reflections" at the end of each chapter, and don't continue until you understand what you want your relationship with the Church to be. If you aren't clear, you are setting yourself up for a lot of pain and confusion when leaders strike back at the initiatives for reform. When you understand and accept within you the truth and spirit of those reflections, and decide to act, turn the page. For those of you old enough to understand the analogy: it's time for the E-Ticket ride! (When Disneyland first opened its doors in Anaheim, the E-Ticket offered you access to the best and fastest rides in the park.)

Expanding Your Knowledge
Father Donald Cozzens, *The Changing Face of the Priesthood.* Father Cozzens contends that upward of 50 percent of Roman Catholic priests have a homosexual orientation. Should the Church exclude the commitment and dedication of these men, it would be unlikely to meet the service needs of their communities. [2]

Margaret Heffernan, *Willful Blindness: Why We Ignore the Obvious at Our Peril* (2011). The author uses the abuse scandal and describes the reasons why the controlling environment of Rome and a culture of denial and protection allowed the abuse to go on for so long. [3]

CHAPTER 6

A PATH TO REFORM

Never be afraid to try something new. Remember, amateurs built the ark; professionals built the Titanic.
— AUTHOR UNKNOWN

To paraphrase Edmund Burke, the hierarchy of the Church has usurped more power than a good man should want or a bad man should have. Implementing a reform strategy to wrest that power away from the institution and place it in the hands of the People of God will not be easy, and it will probably divide most Christian Catholic communities. To keep the status quo leaves people dependent and walking in a rut that has been described as "a grave open on both ends."

The erosion between the bishops and Catholic membership is becoming more evident. In a survey commissioned by the *National Catholic Reporter* and printed in the October 28–November 10, 2011 issue, the following results were reported by Fr. Richard McBrien, the Crowley-O'Brien Professor of Theology at the University of Notre Dame.

- On the matter of Catholic attitudes toward the credibility of the bishops' teachings, the survey found that relatively few Catholics look to church leaders as the sole moral arbiters. This is particularly true with regard to official teachings on such issues as divorce and remarriage, abortion, non-marital sex, homosexuality and contraception.

- More than of half of those surveyed say that individuals, not the hierarchy, are best equipped to make moral decisions on these matters. When it comes to contraception, however, the percentage rises to two-thirds.

- On issues other than divorce and remarriage and contraception (where the percentage of dissidents is roughly the same today as it was 25 years ago), the share of Catholics who look solely to church leaders for guidance on matters of right and wrong has declined.

- Those who attend Mass every week are more inclined to look to the hierarchy for guidance, but not by much. Indeed, half of the oldest generation of Catholics believes individuals themselves are the proper locus of moral authority, even on such issues as abortion.

In summary, on most of the issues the survey asked about, majorities of Catholics said that moral authority rests with individuals, not with the bishops. Given the findings of this survey, it's clear that relatively few Catholics look to the bishops themselves as the sole source of guidance on moral issues.

It is now estimated that 92 percent of Catholic women of childbearing age have used birth control. It doesn't appear that this teaching holds much relevance to women. Bishops and priests are losing credibility on moral issues when they impose the solution and punishment on people who face challenging life problems. If they were taught to educate, facilitate, and counsel, and then leave the solution to the individual without judgment or punishment, they would enhance their role as ministers of the gospel.

NB: Before we discuss the elements of reform, it was suggested to me that there may be some people who want to continue to go to Church and participate in the rituals, but already feel inwardly emancipated from clerical authority. If they don't have the time, energy, or desire to do the work of reform, my hope is they consider participation in the effort, at a minimum, by closing their wallets, and giving those involved the leverage they need to get the bishops to listen.

Levers for Reform

For our purposes here, a *lever* is something used to exert pressure on someone to act in a particular way. Before we get to strategies for change, let's look at the key leverage points that may force open dialogue with the hierarchy to shift away from the current style of Church governance. The degree of influence and impact of each lever would vary according to circumstance.

Money. The Church doesn't exist as a viable institution without donations. One diocese I consulted with gets 90 percent of its operating revenue from the Sunday collection. If that revenue stream were to dry up or be directed toward a parishioner-controlled bank account, it might bring the players to the negotiating table more quickly.

Media savvy. The last thing the Church wants, given its recent problems, is to be in the news. Twenty-four-hour, news-hungry networks need to be fed, and parishioners can work together to tap some of that news time with a strategy for publicity that keeps issues at the top of the hour.

Internet community action. Social media tools such as Facebook and Twitter make a mobilization of national action throughout the Christian Catholic community possible. The overthrow of the Egyptian and Libyan regimes are examples of the effectiveness of these technologies.

Parishioner smarts. Most parishes have intellectual and professional talent among their laity with the ability to put together strategies for reform and with the business acumen to run multimillion-dollar service operations. The question laypeople should be asking is, "If we own this parish, why would we let others run it?" From that question arises another: "Why don't we own it? We paid for it." Most communities have some very smart lawyers who could tie up the closing of parishes for years until the question of ownership is resolved.

Need for urgent change. The key leverage point is people's need and desire for change. Without a critical mass of people willing to take on the hierarchy and challenge its authority over people's lives, any reform is unlikely. Let me give you an example of the urgency I believe is necessary for the laity in one diocese. As I write this paragraph, a news story has just broken that Bishop Finn of the Diocese of Kansas, St. Joseph, has allowed a priest to continue his duties while knowing the priest had taken lewd pictures of parish girls. The bishop was indicted and the priest arrested.

For nine years, the Church has had a policy of zero tolerance of child abuse. If a bishop won't act quickly to enforce that policy, the laity of the diocese must take legal action to expel that bishop and priest from their community. If the laity can't see the need for urgency and action in this case, then the self-serving protection system we discussed earlier will continue to allow some clergy to harm those whom they were ordained to serve. It will also continue to protect the hierarchy from accountability for its actions.

Confidence. Confidence within reformers is essential as they take on the organizational Church they are trying to improve. Confidence allows courage to emerge from within and shifts the challenge from merely finding *a path to reform* to creating *a path of insistence* for that reform. Reform will tolerate nothing less than initiatives that distribute power and authority among the People of God, not only for the sake of the institution, but also for their own spiritual lives. Why are confidence and courage so important? Because the Church hierarchy will fight back with every weapon at its disposal, especially excommunication. *If you can't stand the thought of being excommunicated, then the thought that you will ever be responsible for your own spirituality and oneness with God will forever be in doubt.*

Insistence on cultural change. Literature on organization development contends that to change the culture of an organization, you need the leadership to change—or you need to change the leadership. Culture is defined primarily as "the way we do things around here". Those who have the power to determine the way we do things are the bishop of a diocese, and clergy of the parish. Parishioners either need to select their leaders or get the current leaders to change their attitudes and behaviors so they support the principles of authorship, partnership, and collaborative organizations. Since the latter point isn't likely in the current Church culture, the culture will need to change with the arrival of new and courageous lay leadership.

I'm sure you can come up with other leverage points that can add to the force for change. Remember, you don't always have to win the point to succeed. The implementation of leverage can make it sufficiently uncomfortable for the other person to adjust his position. Early in my career, I worked for Kaiser Medical Care Program in Hawaii. There was a story going around at the time: When the Kaiser health care plan was just beginning in Hawaii, there was a labor dispute with one of the unions, and employees were picketing the entrance to the hospital and clinic. The Kaiser negotiator felt he had a strong argument for his position and wouldn't budge from his offer. Henry Kaiser was off the island at the time and was being kept informed of only the financial issues. When he returned and saw the pickets in front of the hospital, he called the Kaiser negotiator and told him to settle the dispute immediately. He had established a strong relationship with the unions, who were a political force in Hawaii. Since he was trying to establish his health plan with union support, he didn't want his dispute with them advertised by pickets walking in front of his hospital. The pickets were gone the next morning, and the dispute was settled.

The story shows that the players in any conflict have boundaries around their position that they are unlikely to move. This applies to people who want change as well as those who resist change. The key is to understand the soft underbelly of suffering and/or loss that both the people who work on reform and the people who run the institution seek to avoid at all cost. This is the place where movement is possible. For the leaders of the Church, it is the loss of power and control. For the reformers, it's the exclusion from their religious community and fear for their soul. That's why you need to do the work of personal liberation before you take on the hierarchical organization. Otherwise, your own fear will be used against you.

The Stages of Strategic Reform

John Kotter, a professor at Harvard University and a leader in developing strategies for large organizational change, wrote one of the better books on reorganization, leadership, and systemic change in the corporate world. I can't do justice to his scholarship in this brief overview, so I highly recommend that you read *Leading Change* [1] and get a feel for the challenges and opportunities of any significant change effort. Using his framework, I'll describe the approach I would use in starting an initiative for diocesan and parish reform on a large scale. Although I can predict the reaction from the clergy, the "loyal laity", and numerous legal challenges that will impede each step, I'm going to assume that the results we describe in each stage can happen, and therefore give you an example of what might be possible. However, this is a very brief glimpse of a process that requires skilled leadership, adaptive processes to meet unexpected challenges, and significant resources to sustain the effort.

I will break each of the eight stages into three components: The first (A) will answer the question related to the stage; the second (B) will develop the rationale; and the third (C) will identify initiatives to move the reform forward. This overview is very cursory, and an actual change effort will be much more involved. Hopefully, it will provide a sense of the challenge.

John Kotter's Eight-Stage Change Process

1. *Establish a sense of urgency.* What do you need to do to establish a business case and build a sense of urgency for the change effort?

A. Members of national organizations who have worked hard over the years and challenged the unilateral decision making of bishops and pastors can lead this effort. The facts easily make a case for the urgent need for change: millions of dollars are being wasted in settling lawsuits, and bishops are closing parishes to cut expenses. In short, clerical stewardship of assets is abysmal. A recent example involves parishioners who are being sued by the Roman Catholic Diocese of Springfield, Massachusetts. Members of the parish held a peaceful, one-hundred-day vigil inside Mater Dolorosa Church in Holyoke to petition the bishop not to close the church. The suit by the diocese sought their removal from the building by civil authorities. Here a bishop is using civil authority to impose his will, an authority most bishops involved in the abuse scandal didn't recognize when it came to the protection of children. If the additional examples of incompetence, arrogance, and abuse of positional power that are frequent in the media don't wake up the Catholics of the country, I don't know what will.

B. Without a critical mass of people moving with one intention and one voice to correct wrongs, inertia can take over. This is why a clear rationale and statement of urgency is critical in guiding a large group to action. The fatigue that comes from trying to deal with passive resistance used by the Church can be overwhelming. That's why broad-based resistance from the many and closing off the revenue stream are necessary to bring the players to the negotiating table. It will be akin to certain aspects of the Occupy movement that spread through the country in 2011 and the Arab Spring that toppled dictators in the Middle East.

C. Convene a conference of every organization that has tried to make headway toward reform in its particular areas of interest—for example, Call to Action, Voice of the Faithful, CORPUS, Leadership Conference of Women Religious, and many others listed under the banner of Catholic Organizations for Renewal (COR). Prior to the conference, select a coalition of reformers to draft a document that spells out the intentions and urgent case for change. Present this "straw dog" document to the members for discussion and improvement. The meeting should conclude with a consensus statement and action steps to generate further initiatives. The statement should be strong enough and controversial enough to garner national media attention.

2. *Create the guiding coalition.* Who should be leading this change effort, and what is needed to get them onboard and to operate as a team?

A. Personal maturity and commitment necessary to stay with the effort should be major criteria for leadership. Since the people who lead the different reform organizations are dedicated to their specific core mission, it will be necessary to select people who can agree to share talent, time, and financial resources, as well as to prioritize actions that will benefit the greatest good. The leaders should represent each of the constituent groups, with every organization participating directly or indirectly in the evolution of the strategic initiatives. Whether the constituents operate as a team will be dependent on their success with the next step, which includes the realization that they can't do this alone.

B. None of the individual organizations under COR has sufficient membership or finances to take on this reform effectively. I believe the effort will consume millions of dollars in education, publicity, and legal challenges, and will take at least seven years of sustained action with no guarantee the reform initiatives will be achieved under the current organization called the Roman Catholic Church. That is a realistic assessment based on organizational change theory and the recalcitrance of the Church leadership.

C. Every reform organization needs to call its members together and determine whether it wants to join forces with other groups to reform the Church, even though its specific agenda may not be addressed as a priority. For example, if the priority was the ordination of women, would those wanting to end a celibate male priesthood provide the resources to support this initiative, knowing it may delay their priority of a married clergy? All of those involved will together select the initiatives that have the best chance of succeeding in the shortest possible time, with the best use of resources, in a way that builds a strong platform for the next reform. We will discuss the process for developing these issues and priorities, whatever they may be, in the next stage.

3. *Developing a vision and strategies.* What is the best method for creating a shared vision for this change effort, and what elements do you want to see included in the vision?

A. The process of developing a vision statement can be a wordsmith's nightmare as people haggle over the specific ideas they want included in the statement. The time and energy taken to do this work well pays off immeasurably, because this document will keep the team on course and consistent with its core values. One process I've used successfully is called "working back from perfect." I ask people on the leadership team to envision a time when they will be celebrating results together over a glass of wine and are discussing their reform achievements. I ask them to describe the people, initiatives, goals, values, resources, roadmap, and so on that were necessary to achieve their success. In developing this book, I had a group of close friends sit around my dining room table and pepper me with their ideas about the themes, intent, goal, title, and even the cover of the book before I put a word on the page. This is an energizing and supportive process for people leading difficult reforms.

B. As stated many times, "If you don't know where you are going, any road will get you there." It's essential that you have a vision document based on core values and articulated in a format easily understood and widely disseminated. The strategic initiatives to fulfill the vision are generated from this document and are key to guiding the prioritization and use of resources. Also, when resistance or conflict surfaces either from within or outside the reform, this is the document that will refocus the people and the work.

C. From the conference of core reform groups, a subcommittee of the guiding coalition interviews the participating organizations and determines which key elements of each particular vision could be included in an "umbrella" vision statement. Conferencing technology can enable participants countrywide to achieve a vision statement more quickly. If this important task is attempted "on the cheap," precious time will be wasted. And given the age of most of the reformers, the movement would be in jeopardy of losing its leadership, wisdom, and experience.

4. *Communicating the change vision.* What are the best ways to communicate the business case and vision, and how can the leadership team demonstrate commitment to the change effort?

A. Fortunately, we live in a time when the communication of reform isn't limited to a nail, hammer, and ninety-five theses attached to a church door in Wittenberg. The Internet can spread a wild fire of information, and galvanize people to action if they believe in the vision, intentions, and core values of the reform. The leadership must ensure that the message is clear, accurately disseminated, and backed by a strong publicity campaign that keeps it in the public forum until the hierarchy can no longer ignore it.

B. This is a critical stage. The Church's primary response to conflict it can't control is a strategy of passive aggression aimed at wearing down the reformers. When faced with this conflict response, reformers can be discouraged, frustrated, and prone to passive politeness. The reform of the Church needs to be peaceful but not without conflict. The leadership team needs to call for aggressive actions to keep the vision and business case in the public forum to keep its reform constituents in place and in play. *If you lose momentum, you lose the coalition, you lose the critical mass, and you lose.*

C. Hire experts in media, advertising, and running political campaigns to forge the vision statement, strategic initiatives, and core value messages in ways that will stick in the public consciousness. Then put on a media blitz equivalent to a full court press used in basketball. The full court press strategy will work only if those putting on the "press" have the physical and financial stamina to outrun and outlast the opponent. Cut off the revenue stream and see if that moves the discussion in a more effective way; file injunctions to stop building projects; and record priests' sermons around election time to see if they're violating the separation of church and state clause of the Constitution by advocating for or disparaging a candidate.

5. *Empowering broad-based action.* What obstacles need to be removed, and how can you encourage risk taking and innovative solutions?

A. The obstacles that need removing are, for the most part, personal. Remove the fear of excommunication, and replace it with original blessing, authorship, and personal responsibility for one's spiritual life. Educate and support parishioners in removing their fear of and dependence on the clergy, and help them develop responsibility for their own moral choices and processes for forgiveness. The legal obstacles are significant but depend on how far reformers want to take the asset control issues of the Church. Finally, archaic dogma, canon law, and erroneous theological concepts need to be challenged.

B. I have never liked the term *empower*, because it can connote someone else giving you power so you can act. I use the word *encourage.* If we encourage one another and support one another in looking within to find the courage to act, the intellect and emotional maturity of the individual can remove the psychological obstacles. Even if the leadership falters on reform, individuals can choose to move forward with their own action to remain free of the control and punishment system of the Church.

C. Invite theologians and like-minded clergy to join the reform and solidify the foundation for the initiatives with a personal, professional, and organizational rationale for change. In his recent book, *The Pope's War*, Matthew Fox lists twenty-five initiatives for reforming and/or breaking from the Church. There are many good ideas in the list, but they will wither without a critical mass of people organized under one banner and voice insisting on change. I recommend Fox's list as a starting point to formulate the vision and strategic initiatives outlined in the previous steps.

6. *Generating short-term wins.* How can you generate some quick wins early in the change effort, and what can you do to leverage their momentum?

A. After you get the vision statement and key initiatives into the public arena, let the document cause a renewal of the conversation and start surfacing the issues that the Church is trying to suppress. Once this is accomplished, ask for donations to an LLP (Limited Liability Corporation) set up in every diocese and run by laypeople. Ask people to send their Sunday donations to this organization rather than giving it to their local parish.

B. All corporations need profit to continue their services to customers. Even non-profits need more than their current expenses to invest in new technology, services, and salary increases. When you interrupt a diocese's ability to pay its debts, its ability to borrow is affected, thereby putting it at risk of bankruptcy. This inhibits its ability to serve parishioners, provide houses of worship, and forces a confrontation where the playing field is more balanced.

C. Now is the time for lawyers to take the stage. With money from donations to the LLP, sue the diocese for the return of the property that parishioners have paid for. Lawyers need to provide a legal basis and process where the assets are returned and managed by the laity. The LLP will continue to fund the charitable works of the parishes, but not expend a dollar to pay mortgages, salaries, or debts and expenses associated with parishes until asset reform is achieved. The short-term win here is the determination of whether a legal strategy is possible for laity to gain ownership of the assets. If it isn't, the strategy shifts to a legal means to force the bishop and pastors to include laity in the management of the properties and assets without a veto by a pastor or bishop.

7. *Consolidating gains and producing more change.* How can you capture the synergy from parallel projects as well as alter other systems, processes, and policies to ensure the success of the envisioned change?

A. Answering this question assumes two achievements. The first is a shift of control of assets from clergy to laity, whereby the laity run parishes and dioceses in partnership with the priest or bishop. This partnership may be an initial "all we could get legally" win, that has neither group with unilateral control over the retention or distribution of assets or over personnel. The second is the acceptance of a theology of inclusion that never prevents a qualified person from assuming any role of service to the community if invited to do so by the community. If lay and clergy alike support these two goals, you can begin to assimilate parallel projects, such as married clergy and the ordination of women.

B. Without progress here, the initiatives fail and the Church returns to business as usual. The reason therapists recommend you take at least one step toward overcoming your fear on the first try is that failure builds internal resistance to trying again. If this attempt to change is going to work, it needs to be backed by sufficient resources and sustained by a succession of committed leaders so the first steps build momentum that's sustained until the goal is achieved. The notion that it's acceptable to go back to the pre-Vatican II days of governance and lay dependence on the clergy can't be an option. Given the policies and doctrinal direction of Pope Benedict, if the initiatives falter or fail, the return to a more repressive Church is very possible.

C. If success is achieved here, the doors are open for a Civil Rights model of intervention. Under the umbrella of Catholic Organizations for Renewal, a critical mass of people seeking redress for a variety of grievances can begin campaigns for reform on the same date in the same year. Keep the media pressure on, squeeze the revenue stream, and call a gathering of reformers outside every parish on Sunday morning and outside the diocesan office every day until the bishop responds. Have an action team to coordinate these efforts across every diocese in the nation.

8. *Anchoring new approaches in the culture.* How can you anchor the new approaches in your culture and core business practices?

I have a different view of this last step, so I am consolidating my thoughts as I comment on the rationale and initiatives for anchoring new approaches. The word *anchor* is inappropriate when referring to the Church's reform and renewal. The last thing the Church needs is to keep its reforms *anchored* when you have people to serve whose problems and needs are morphing at the speed of light into different and even more difficult issues. John Kotter wrote about corporate culture and performance, and he suggested that it wasn't necessarily a strong culture that made a company successful or a weak culture that caused its failure. He found that businesses likely to succeed over time had adaptive cultures, among other attributes. In addition to the capacity to shift quickly and deftly to meet the demands of customers, successful businesses had leaders who demanded from their people the final characteristic in the POP diagnostic: the willingness to change. These companies were likely to thrive in the marketplace. In the Church, the lack of adaptation is impeded by dogma or canon law whose interpretation of and application to modern-day problems is so rigid that it ceases to support individuals struggling with difficult life problems. As a result, the gospel invitation to welcome all who are burdened is seriously limited, and leaves the doors open for members to exit and seek support elsewhere.

Kotter's model of structuring change is only one approach for organizations to consider as they seek to remain relevant in the marketplace. Other options, depending on how they are led and managed, can be more divisive or confrontational to the stakeholders. They range from a "greenfield," which begins by starting over and building anew, to "island hopping" that starts with one entity of an organization, like a division in a major corporation, and works the reforms in that division. Depending on the effectiveness of results, it then transports the successful change initiatives to the next division. In the Church example, you would start with one parish and innovate reforms until all parishes in the diocese were involved. The goal, regardless of the strategy used, is that all hierarchy and clergy feel the insistence of the People of God to renew, evolve, reform—to change.

Whatever change strategy is used, it should include the following criteria:

1. Those engaged in the reform agree that the selected strategy and initiatives will move the renewal forward toward stated goals and fulfillment of the vision.
2. Positional leadership authority serves and supports those acting with the authority of knowledge and skill.
3. All involved are aware of and support the principles of authorship, partnership, and collaborative organization.
4. Nonviolence is the basis of all actions, even though insistence towards results may cause a violent response.
5. All initiatives are well resourced with staff, finances, media access, office availability, communication technology, and supplies.

Deciding to Be Involved in Reform

There's enough information and material throughout this book to get the Christian Catholic community started on the shifts we have discussed. The question everyone must ask now is, "Am I willing to work to reform this Church, especially if I don't need it for my sense of spirituality or community?" I don't have the answer to this question, because it must reside in each of us. If out of a love, appreciation, or commitment for the positive aspects of your Catholic experience, you decide to lead or be involved in reform, be aware of the cost to you personally, professionally, and organizationally. If you commit to do it effectively, your life will change forever, and you will find yourself way outside your comfort zone—and quite possibly way outside the traditional church you have known as Catholic.

Historians regard Teddy Roosevelt as one of our greater presidents. He earned this accolade in no small measure due to the corporate interests he took on, so that the average citizen could get a "Square Deal," the term he used to describe his domestic agenda. Many working to solve the problems in our current financial house of cards would welcome his presence. He was able to achieve much, not primarily because of the power of his office, but because he was engaged in life and used his values, desires, and talents to provide people with opportunities.

In the reflection below, Roosevelt speaks of engagement in a great worthy effort. I direct his words to the many people who sit at services and enjoy the ritual that confirms their childhood experience of Church, who seek the status quo, the comfort of noninvolvement, and the distance and safety of being a bystander. See if his words encourage you to reconsider and choose involvement rather than the status quo. Although you may not choose it for your own sake, consider using some of your time, talent, or treasure for the sake of the children and future generations.

Reflection

"It is not the critic who counts; not the man who points out how the strong man stumbles, or where the doer of deeds could have done them better. The credit belongs to the man who is actually in the arena, whose face is marred by dust and sweat and blood; who strives valiantly; who errs, who comes short again and again, because there is no effort without error and shortcoming; but who does actually strive to do the deeds; who knows great enthusiasms, the great devotions; who spends himself in a worthy cause; who at the best knows in the end the triumph of high achievement, and who at the worst, if he fails, at least fails while daring greatly, so that his place shall never be with those cold and timid souls who neither know victory nor defeat." [2]

This book's opportunity for education and reflection draws to a close. However, there is a wealth of information still available for every barrier or challenge you encounter. If it isn't in a book or on Kindle, search your own mind and heart, for the answer is surely there with a little courage, exploration, and choice making.

The final chapter will summarize the key points in the book so you have a shorthand guide to remember the gift you are and the responsibility you hold for your own life. Let's create and integrate a new approach for thinking and being as we consider the term *Christian Catholic*.

Expanding Your Knowledge

I recommend you read two of John Kotter's books, *Leading Change* (1995) and *A Sense of Urgency* (2008), [3] to get a realistic sense of the challenge ahead. Remember, you are taking on the largest religious organization in the world.

Matthew Fox, *The Pope's War* (2011). The twenty-five initiatives in the back of this book will give you ideas consistent with your sense of authorship and the basis for some reform initiatives. However, be sure to link them to a strong change model. [4]

CHAPTER 7

AWAKEN

*Don't be trapped by dogma, which is living
with the results of other people's thinking.*
— STEVE JOBS, STANFORD COMMENCEMENT
ADDRESS, 2005

In *Hamlet*, Shakespeare wrote what is probably the key question for all of us to address if we want to live life to the fullest: "To be or not to be, that is the question." [1] This simple line directs all of us to wake up to the potential of the life we have. It also challenges us to choose whether to live it controlled by others' thinking or to explore life beyond the boundaries of our own beliefs and current experiences. The Church would have you believe it has the truth and solutions for your life. You have to decide if you want to live by its dogma, and in so doing, stop the growth and exploration of your being and existence, and reject the notion of total responsibility for your life.

Reading this book may have led you to doubt your faith in the Church and its role in your life. If that has happened— good! The doubt you experience gives you the chance to explore. However, don't allow doubt to force you to run to another external source so you can return to certainty. Doubt allows the opportunity for new truth and experiences to enter your life and challenge your certainty.

I have a friend who is so certain of everything that he defends his ignorance with the passion of one who is afraid of losing his worldview and his significant relationships. He grabs hold and tries to control everything and everyone in his life. He doesn't have an alternative to his current state because he doesn't trust the mind and heart experience of exploration. He doesn't know he is an original blessing and lovable; he doesn't own his own problems; he doesn't forgive; and he doesn't recognize or explore the pain in his heart caused by his family of origin. He could be the spokesperson for the phrase "Seldom right, but never in doubt." While thinking and caring about him, I adapted the model on consciousness to help awaken in each of us the process for getting unstuck, for opening our minds and hearts to the opportunity of living with a sense of purpose, peace, and love.

My exploration process took many years, with the most important part being my marriage to my wife, Patti. One evening we were at dinner with close friends when our hostess asked me where I grew up. Without missing a beat, Patti said, "He was raised in San Jose, but he grew up with me!" The truth of that statement is evident to all our close friends, and the process of our "growing up" together was exploratory and quite messy at times. If you decide to reevaluate your growing up process in the Church, you may want to start with acknowledging that you are free from anyone else's dogma.

Summary

Whether you agree with what I've written, my hope is you begin with a new consciousness about your relationship with the Church. I ask that, if you agree with my statements or process, let it be a beginning for the continuation of your own search. If you don't agree, listen to your resistance and ask these simple questions: "How did I learn to resist this notion, and from whom did I learn it?" Your willingness to answer these questions will allow you to learn from whom the belief was generated, whether you now own the belief as an adult, and whether it supports the learning that affirms you as a loving human being worthy of support, love, and life while walking this planet.

The process of growing in consciousness requires that you question the current state of your awareness around any given issue. The issue might be your marriage, your children, the way you work and act in the world, or an addiction. The process walks you through an awareness of your current consciousness to possibilities, to choice, to action, to consequences, to a new consciousness. Examples of how you can utilize this process are in the following summary of this book's key points:

Consciousness. The new awareness that this book asks you to consider comes from a shift in thinking about who you are. It suggests that you are

☑ an original blessing rather than a person born in to a state of spiritual alienation called original sin.

☑ a person who can choose to own the problem rather than deflecting or blaming someone else for a negative experience or giving the problem to an institution like the Church to solve.

☑ a person who, in accepting the responsibility for forgiving yourself, can extend forgiveness to others.

As your beliefs evolve about your unconditional lovability and as you acknowledge your purpose, knowledge, and skills, the awakening continues and increases your awareness that you are a person

☑ with a sense of and commitment to personal authorship—defined as the recognition and acceptance of one's value, knowledge, skill, and commitment as it relates to any purpose, goal or task—and the acceptance of accountability for any outcomes that result from the exercise of your power and authority.

☑ who can develop significant relationships based on partnership. Partnership requires a relationship that's mutually accepted and renewed by two or more people whose purpose is to commit their personal authorship in the achievement of an agreed-upon goal. The rights, responsibilities, and potential consequences are identified based on mutual agreement and commitment, and are shared equally or equitably depending on contribution.

Possibilities. A new consciousness of who you are now allows for possibilities or options that you can generate and expand beyond those mentioned here:

☑ You are free from dependency on the Church, its doctrine, and its ministers.

☑ You can expand your knowledge and experience to other spiritual disciplines that enhance your understanding and meaning of the gospel.

☑ You can build collaborative organizations to reform the current institution and make it more Christian than Catholic.

☑ You can leave the Church; you can stay in the Church; you can stay in the Church, but in a very different way than you did in the Church of your childhood; or you can ignore everything that's in this book.

Choices. You are aware that no one "does" your life other than you, because you alone ultimately choose your response to all experiences you encounter. You can now choose to do any of the following:

☑ Grieve the known certainty of childhood beliefs taught by the Church.

☑ Develop your own spirituality while always being open to new knowledge that adds to the truth of your life.

☑ Assess the role of the Church in your life and whether it's a resource for your growth or a barrier that impedes it—or something in between.

☑ Be involved in the reform of the institutional Church for your own sake as well as for the sake of your children and of those it has injured.

Actions. Choice without action is like having a great business plan that's never executed. It never makes a dime for anyone, except the consultant who helped put it together. New consciousness requires new action; otherwise, the awareness can erode into internal conflict, rationalization that seeks to avoid the truth or emotional withdrawal that can result in depression. Even the choice not to act can take you back to a state of emotional dependence. Remember this definition by Alfred Einstein: "Insanity is doing the same thing over and over again, and expecting a different result." A new awareness in your relationship with the Church requires new choices in thought, feelings, and behaviors.

Actions arising from the new consciousness awakened by this book may cause you to determine the following:

☑ You always go to communion regardless of what Church rules say. You need to follow your own conscience on issues of divorce, contraception, living in a loving committed relationship regardless of sexual orientation, and other issues of conscience.

☑ You always forgive yourself first, and then you offer forgiveness to the person with whom you are experiencing conflict. If you decide later that you want to confess, you use the priest only for education, consultation, or facilitation if you respect his authority of knowledge and skill. You know he doesn't have authority of position nor can he impose a penance that relieves you of your responsibility for forgiveness of the one harmed.

☑ You can close your checkbook as a leverage to help others who are working on reforms to bring the Church into alignment with the gospel and with current organizational practices that distribute power and authority among those most capable in the community.

☑ You can leave the Church, stay in the Church, or stay but show up in a very different way.

☑ You commit to a lifelong effort to affirm your unconditional lovability as a person who can, through forgiveness, love unconditionally without the need or expectation of return.

☑ You can, as St. Francis said, "Preach the gospel at all times, sometimes use words."

Consequences. Newton's third law of motion states, "For every action there is an equal and opposite reaction." Should you decide to work on the organizational reform we discussed in chapter six, A Path to Reform, be prepared for a not-so-equal-and-opposite reaction from the Church. The reaction may be harsh and come as an attempt to alienate, isolate, or excommunicate you from the Catholic community. The final fear card used by Church authorities is the threat that you are risking your salvation. But salvation is in your hands. Your awareness of your original blessing; your acceptance that problems belong to you to resolve; and that the power to forgive yourself and others is embedded within your humanity; clearly supports any understanding one might have of a concept of spiritual salvation. Don't use the belief that God will solve your problems, thereby undermining the faith you have in yourself to resolve them. The loving God within is already working your life with you.

Not all consequences need be negative, especially if you come to a deepening awareness about your need for a Christian community rather than for a traditional Roman Catholic Church community. Whether you find that community in a subculture of parish life within the Catholic Church or outside it, the spirit within will guide you to the change you request. Martin Marty, a professor at the University of Chicago, was once asked, "Does God answer prayer?" He replied, "Not the prayer of the ego, but the intent of one's soul." So seek the intent of your soul, and may it involve the search to find the peace and love that comes with the blessings of a fully engaged and meaningful life.

New Consciousness

And so it continues until your last breath—that process and experience of learning your truth about yourself and growing in your awareness of the amazing gift you are to all those who cross your path. I think Søren Kierkegaard, the Danish philosopher and theologian, spoke of this ongoing search for a new consciousness when he wrote;

"Do not interrupt the flight of your soul; do not distress what is best in you; do not enfeeble your spirit with half wishes and half thoughts. Ask yourself and keep on asking until you find the answer, for one may have known something many times, acknowledged it; one may have willed something many times, attempted it—and yet, only the deep inner motion, only the heart's indescribable emotion, only that will convince you that what you have acknowledged belongs to you, that no power can take it from you—for only the truth that builds up, is truth for you." [2]

Conclusion

A friend of mine who has written extensively said the most difficult part of writing is the first sentence, and the second most difficult is the last. The first is the struggle to put the initial words in an order that begins to express what you believe has value and meaning for others. The last part is having the wisdom to know when to stop. I'm looking right now at a box of material that I thought might contribute to the case I tried to make: that personal and institutional change evolves from the inside out. I decided to put the box away until my Muse guides me to take up the pen again.

So now the focus shifts to you who have read the book. My hope is that it has engaged and inspired you enough to look for whatever support and resources you need to continue your journey. I encourage you to follow the admonition of Dr. Martin Luther King Jr.:

"Take the first step in faith.
You don't have to see the whole staircase,
just take the first step." [3]

I bid you fair winds and calm seas, a safe harbor during turbulent weather, and the joy of exploration beyond the known world of your current experience.

APPENDIX A

FIVE-PHASE PARTNERSHIP DEVELOPMENT AND RENEWAL PROCESS

1. High Energy and High Expectations

It all begins with people who have a commitment to partnership to achieve a goal. This first stage is usually characterized by the following:

- A period of undetermined length filled with enthusiastic yet unsustainable expectations. Facts and data aren't as important as vision, passion, and commitment to the partnership agreement. "Let's get this thing going!"

- Partners' faults or weaknesses are minimized, dismissed, or considered unimportant to the success of the venture. This is a "head in the sand" approach that often happens if a partner who is disruptive brings a lot to the party in the way of expertise or material assets.

2. Conflict and Compromise

This is the first encounter with disappointment and unmet expectations about the partnership. It can lead to observable behavior such as the following:

- Annoyance, anger, or hurt with a partner's habits or use of power.

131

- Rationalization or compromise to deal with interpersonal problems. Partners may attempt to regress to the first stage, where conflict was buried and unpleasant behavior was minimized or excused.

- Attempts to explain a disruptive partner's behavior to confirm one's own perceptions. This process begins "behind the back" communication, which keeps people from openly and directly confronting issues.

- Questions surface about one's role or involvement in the partnership: "What did I get myself into?"

3. Control Response

If partners don't stop and consciously address the first symptoms of conflict, they may revert to coping mechanisms that attempt to control the relationship.

- One or more partners give up their wants and needs to keep the relationship, usually with significant resentment and anger.

- One segment of the partnership might develop unilateral strategies to manipulate another partner to comply or change so that issues don't interfere with goal achievement.

- Compromise of one's authorship is very possible in this stage. The phrase "go along to get along" is a typical response in this stage of conflict.

4. Partnership Assessment and Separation

This stage is based on confronting the members' wants, needs, and expectations. Truth telling is key; partners need to come clean and speak their truth about their level of satisfaction with the partnership. When partners recognize they are going to face other partners' ongoing limitations or a lack of satisfaction with the partnership, they must deal with the issues honestly and productively. Otherwise, separation or letting go in some form is inevitable. When partners refuse to cope with the struggles or to let go of impediments to the relationship, they separate in one of the following ways:

- Staying but withdrawing (disengaging)

- Staying with increased unresolved conflict (drama)

- Staying with plans to leave at the first possible moment (unspoken exit strategy)

- Leaving physically but holding on to emotionally (internal drama on a continual loop)

- Leaving physically and emotionally (don't want to play anymore)

The separation struggle ends when the partnership is dissolved or the partners choose to recommit. At this stage, it's critical for partners to address their sense of authorship if it has been lost in the enmeshment of the relationships.

5. Recommitment through Mutual Support

Despite differences and irritations, partners find a compelling reason to be committed to the relationship and its purpose. The relationship is renewed because each partner is willing to adapt and to problem solve unacceptable behavior that impedes goal achievement. Finally, partners cease to think and talk about dissolving the partnership. They are in this through thick and thin. This is a time of significant personal and partnership growth facilitated by regular feedback that is positive, constructive, and goal affirming. Partners explore the following:

- New communication and support systems

- Ways for individuals to work on and change habits and traits that are impediments to goal achievement

- Support systems that minimize the impact of differences on the relationship

- Creative options to express personal authorship while achieving the stated purpose

APPENDIX B

CHARACTERISTICS OF LOW-PERFORMANCE TEAMS

- Goals are unclear, and the stated results are neither challenging nor compelling. (This impedes personal excellence.)

- Resources are inadequate or poorly used. (The goal doesn't drive resource allocation or distribution.)

- Membership is static, and individuals stay on when they are no longer contributing or needed. (Team membership is guaranteed, regardless of relevance to the goal.)

- Necessary resources aren't brought on when required. ("Just in time"—getting resources and material to the activity when actually needed—is ignored or poorly executed.)

- Only the one who holds positional authority exercises leadership. (The Leadership that comes from knowledge and skill is subject to veto by the one who holds positional authority. Bureaucratic policy and practice drives decision making.)

- Individual members have minimal ownership and commitment to the goal. (Personal excellence is not in the equation for motivational behavior.)

- Communication is based on blame or self-preservation; conflict usually arises out of nonproductive argument rather than for the sake of challenge and resolution. (People protect themselves over the team.)

APPENDIX C

CHARACTERISTICS OF HIGH-PERFORMANCE TEAMS

- The articulation of a challenging goal that, if achieved, adds value to the work community, customers, or stakeholders, and provides a reward that enhances the personal, professional, or organizational life of those who participate.

- The team is formed by a goal advocate(s) who selects people with knowledge, skill, and commitment to the goal.

- A goal advocate(s), team members, and stakeholders develop and sustain goals and initiatives, and customers are included, at some level, in the development and/or execution of the initiatives.

- The plan for achievement of the goal is based on non-competitive, author/partner principles with strategies, structures, and systems in alignment with those principles.

- Those in leadership with the authority of position are in service to those in a leadership role that comes with the authority of knowledge and skill.

- The choice to stay in the team is dependent on commitment to the goal as well as the willingness and qualifications of the team member to contribute to the milestones and to have her or his progress and contribution toward the goal evaluated by other members.

- All support functions and disciplines are in service to the goal.

- There is no punishment for telling the truth; there is no tolerance for deception.

- Results are evaluated on criteria relevant to resource investment, profitability, expense allocation, and on the level of commitment to stakeholders, organization members, and customers.

REFERENCE NOTES

Introduction
1. Carl Jung: Swiss psychiatrist, Psychologist and Founder of Analytic Psychology, 1875-1961. Quote from http://www.Thinkexist.com

Chapter 1: Changing from the Inside Out
1. Father Donald Cozzens, *The Changing Face of the Priesthood.* (Collegeville Minnesota: The Liturgical Press, 2000).

2. Bart Ehrman, *Misquoting Jesus: The story behind who changed the Bible and why,* (New York, Harper Collins, 2005).

3. James Carroll, *Constantine's Sword, The Church and the Jews.* (New York, Houghton Mifflin Co., 2001).

Chapter 2: Thinking Outside the Nine Dots
1. Matthew Fox, *Original Blessing.* (Santa Fe, New Mexico: Bear & Company, 1983). Path 1 Theme 2 p 47.

2. Professor Herbert Haag as quoted by Matthew Fox, *Original Blessing.* (Santa Fe, New Mexico: Bear & Company, 1983). Path 1 Theme 2 p 47.

3. Professor Herbert Haag as quoted by Matthew Fox, *Original Blessing.* (Santa Fe, New Mexico: Bear & Company, 1983). Path 1 Theme 2 p 47.

4. Matthew Fox, *Original Blessing*. (Santa Fe, New Mexico: Bear & Company, 1983). Path 1 Theme 2 p 47.

5. Hans Kung, *On Being a Christian*, (New York, Doubleday, 1976). pp 313-316.

6. Matthew Fox, *Original Blessing*, (Santa Fe, New Mexico: Bear & Company, 1983). Path 1 Theme 2 p 49.

7. Matthew Fox, *Original Blessing*, (Santa Fe, New Mexico: Bear & Company, 1983).

8. John D. Crossan & Richard Watts, *Who is Jesus*, (Louisville, Kentucky: John Knox Press, 1969).

Chapter 3: Authorship

1. Rollo May, *Power & Innocence A search for the sources of violence*. (New York: W. W. Norton & Company1998). pp 105-109.

2. William James: American Philosopher and Psychologist, leader of the philosophical movement called Pragmatism. 1842-1910. http://www.Thinkexist.com

3. Victor Frankl, *Man's Search for Meaning* (Boston: Beacon Press, 2006). pp 65-66.

4. Catechism of the Catholic Church: Part 2, Section 2, Chapter 1, Article 1, Statement 1261.

5. Catechism of the Catholic Church: Part 2, Section 2, Chapter 1 Article 1, Statement 1250.

6. Catechism of the Catholic Church: Part II, Section 2, Chapter 1, Article 3, Statement 1415.

7. Catechism of the Catholic Church: Part 1 Section 1 Chapter 2 Article 2 Statement 100.

8. William Blake (28 November 1757 – 12 August 1827) *Songs of Innocence*, 1789. English poet, painter, and printmaker.

9. Marianne Williamson, *A Return to Love*, (New York, Harper Collins 1992). pp 190-191.

10. Sam Keene, *Fire in the Belly, On being a Man*, (New York: Bantam Books 1991). p 12.

11. Carol Tavris and Elliot Aronson, *Mistakes Were Made but Not by Me: Why We Justify Foolish Beliefs, Bad Decisions and Hurtful Acts*, (Harcourt Inc. New York 2007).

12. Albert Ellis and Robert Harper, *A Guide to Rational Living*, (Chatsworth, Wilshire Books 1975).

13. Ekhart Tolle, *The Power of Now*, (Namaste Publishing, Novato 1999).

Chapter 4: Partnership

1. Gandhi; October 2, 1869 – January 30, 1948). Quote from http://www.Thinkexist.com

2. Peter Block, *Stewardship: Choosing Service over Self Interest* (San Francisco Berrett Kohler 1993).

3. William Bridges, *Transitions: Making Sense of Life's Changes*, (Perseus Publishing, 1980).

4. Cynthia Scott and Dennis Jaffe, *Getting Your Organization to Change*, (Menlo Park, Crisp Publications, 1999). (4)

Chapter 5: Collaborative Organizations
1. Peter Block, *Stewardship: Choosing Service over Self Interest* (San Francisco Berrett Kohler1993). p 77.

2. Father Donald Cozzens, *The Changing Face of the Priesthood.* (Collegeville Minnesota, The Liturgical Press, 2000).

3. Margaret Heffernan, *Willful Blindness: Why We Ignore the Obvious at Our Peril*, New York, Walker Publishing, 2011).

Chapter 6: A Path to Reform
1. John Kotter, *Leading Change:* (Boston, Harvard Business School Press 1996). Read all of it!

2. Teddy Roosevelt, Excerpt from speech on, *Citizenship in a Republic*, Paris, 1910).

3. John Kotter, *A sense of Urgency* (Boston, Harvard Business School Press 2008). Read all of it!

4. Matthew Fox, *The Popes War:* (New York, Sterling Publishing, 2011). pp 230-237.

Chapter 7: Awaken
1. Hamlet, Act 3, Scene 1.

2. Søren Kierkegaard, *Either/Or,* 1843 Ultimatum, p 254. http://en.wikiquote.org

3. Dr. Martin Luther King Jr. Quotes.

89280916R00091

Made in the USA
San Bernardino, CA
22 September 2018